▶ **Master-Servant Childhood**

DOI: 10.1057/9781137364791

Other Palgrave Pivot titles

DOI: 10.1057/9781137364791

palgrave▸pivot

Master-Servant Childhood: A History of the Idea of Childhood in Medieval English Culture

Patrick Joseph Ryan

*King's University College at
Western University, Canada*

DOI: 10.1057/9781137364791

© Patrick Joseph Ryan 2013

First published 2013 by
PALGRAVE MACMILLAN

Palgrave Macmillan in the UK is an imprint of Macmillan Publishers Limited, registered in England, company number 785998, of Houndmills, Basingstoke, Hampshire RG21 6XS.

Palgrave Macmillan in the US is a division of St Martin's Press LLC, 175 Fifth Avenue, New York, NY 10010.

Palgrave Macmillan is the global academic imprint of the above companies and has companies and representatives throughout the world.

Palgrave® and Macmillan® are registered trademarks in the United States, the United Kingdom, Europe and other countries.

ISBN: 978–1–137–36480–7 EPUB
ISBN: 978–1–137–36479–1 PDF
ISBN: 978–1–137–36478–4 Hardback

A catalogue record for this book is available from the British Library.

A catalog record for this book is available from the Library of Congress.

www.palgrave.com/pivot

DOI: 10.1057/9781137364791

For libraries and all who keep them

DOI: 10.1057/9781137364791

Contents

DOI: 10.1057/9781137364791

Acknowledgements

My debts to mentors, colleagues and friends are greater than I can count, but I would like to thank three people who read drafts of this book: an Anglo-Saxon scholar and supremely skilled editor – Jane Toswell; a Middle English literary critic and fellow historian of childhood – Dan Kline; and a grant writer, newspaper columnist and supportive spouse – Julie Ryan. Their encouraging questions, constructive criticism and careful editing was invaluable. The remaining mistakes and limitations, of course, are entirely my fault.

DOI: 10.1057/9781137364791

palgrave▶**pivot**

www.palgrave.com/pivot

Wickberg's Door: Childhood and Structures of Thought

Abstract: *The mainline approach toward the history of childhood suffers from two major problems: (1) it has failed to honestly confront epistemological divergences inherent in the field; (2) this smoothing over of differences has fostered an inability to move beyond the "Ariès debate". Examining childhood as structure of thought and feeling takes a clear position on these issues and offers strong reasons for studying childhood historically. The section concludes by outlining the book's argument that childhood in medieval England was embedded within master-servant hierarchies that extended from a sense of being in time (age) as a correspondence between earthly change and eternal order.*

Ryan, Patrick Joseph. *Master-Servant Childhood: A History of the Idea of Childhood in Medieval English Culture.* Basingstoke: Palgrave Macmillan, 2013. DOI: 10.1057/9781137364791.

When I arrived at the University of Texas at Dallas some years ago, I found a lone note pasted to the office door of Dan Wickberg. It read: "The history of childhood is a nightmare from which we have only recently begun to awaken."[1] I could not help but smile. As if J.H. Hexter had put it there, Lloyd deMause's famous thesis was turned against itself by the double-meaning of *history*.[2] No longer a condemnation of the treatment of children in the past, it was a challenge to all those writing history as a means of giving a "voice" to subaltern groups, when taken to its logical extreme – the History of children.

Having founded a global network for the history of childhood (*H-Childhood*) with Kris Lindenmeyer the previous year, I might have mistaken Wickberg's door as a nasty greeting. Welcome to Texas. Yet, there was something more substantial than smirking ridicule behind this door. Wickberg was in the midst of fashioning a critique of social history as the recovery of experience and agency. He would put these ideas together as part of a cogent defence of the history of ideas in a series of influential articles over the next decade.[3] This book approaches childhood as a structure of thought (a discourse) and takes seriously the challenge implicit on Wickberg's door: is the history of childhood a proper field of study, and why would anyone devote themselves to it?

Historical research upon childhood emerged ancillary to other fields of study. In the mid-twentieth century, scholarly concern with generational relations increased with more nuanced understandings of human socialization, and in conjunction with bold, global theories of modernization.[4] Interest in childhood and youth was sustained partly because innovations within socialization theory framed how we understood race, gender, class and national identification.[5] This provided fertile ground to explore a maxim fundamental to the discipline of history: ideas and relationships that seem inevitable or natural are contingent upon some very precise historical developments. Childhood also offered many topical possibilities beyond what previously had been considered the boundary of historical work (juvenile sex crime, prohibitions against child labour, age-consciousness, fear of kidnapping, abhorrence for the child molester).[6] The study of young people could be used to put a twist upon any conceivable inquiry. So, we have historical studies of "coming of age" in Great Britain; during the 1930s; in Buffalo, New York; as a Jewish girl; on the farm; and in pursuit of the American Revolution – among others.[7]

DOI: 10.1057/9781137364791

Initially, historians paid attention to childhood due to the rising profile of socialization theory, and partly because exploring the topic was an obvious way to do something "new" within well-established, saturated fields. Which is to say, that the history of childhood and youth moved according to the shape of a larger intellectual network. One thread within this net coalesced around the idea that histories paying attention to children and youth gave witness to their participation in culture and society, and that this granted a moral status to contemporary young persons. As Harry Hendrick put it, treating children as historical actors makes history "more inclusive, and therefore more democratic".[8] Setting aside the precise meaning (or veracity) of this claim, it fit with an interdisciplinary spectrum of childhood research that arose in opposition to bio-social determinism and romantic sentimentalism.[9] In the late twentieth century, the study of childhood adopted a familiar slogan, found from A to Z across the subject headings of the humanities and social sciences: *children are social actors and childhood is socially constructed.*[10] This was consistent with a cultural-turn among historians during the 1990s, and it worked against efforts to integrate the field with the sciences of developmental psychology and demography.[11] Of course, the best cultural analysis offered more than slogans, or a means for debunking bad science. Studies of childhood and youth gathered around a larger historical interest in the production of human science and the making of a modern self.[12] Interest in child and youth cultures fostered creative uses of archival material and visual evidence, while complicating our understanding of identity, consumer culture, literature and the arts.[13] All the while, the area was closely associated with the study of disability and social policy.[14]

During the late 1990s organizational structures were erected to support the increasingly plausible idea that childhood could be a distinct field of historical work. This movement was aided by the establishment of new electronic networks, academic societies and work-groups, and peer-review journals.[15] Universities in Scandinavia, Canada, the UK and the United States founded programmes and centres dedicated in part, or entirely, to the interdisciplinary historical study of childhood and youth. Organizational development, of course, is no answer to Wickberg's challenge. A reasoned response must examine the intellectual threads that knit the field together, reflect upon their coherence, and assess the quality of the debates that they have produced – or failed to produce.

DOI: 10.1057/9781137364791

One of the most coherent programmatic statement about the emergent field was offered by Martha Saxton in her introduction to the first issue of *The Journal of the History of Childhood and Youth* in 2008: 1) *Age* is an important "category of analysis" like race, class, and gender. 2) Like all sub-altern *social groups*, children's interests are advanced when we "destabliz[e] traditional assumptions about…who" counts historically. 3) *Deterministic* ideas about human development as a linear, universal process, and roman-tic ideals of childhood innocence should be challenged. 4) By giving childhood a history, we will find "children's *agency*", elevate their status as moral actors, and "devis[e] new way[s] to open doors onto the *experience* and imaginations of children".[16]

These four mainline themes should not be granted the status of a "new paradigm" of childhood, but it seems to me that they encapsulate the most widely accepted reasons for pursuing the history of childhood and youth today.[17] Without forgetting the varied, significant contributions that historical study of childhood has made, the current orientation of the field suffers from two major problems. 1) The field has not adequately confronted foundational tensions that are inherent in the mainline themes. 2) As a result, we have not developed fresh, interesting debates about the over-arching historical narrative of childhood and its wider significance. In this matter, the field seems trapped in a tiring, decades-long discussion of Philippe Ariès *Centuries of Childhood*.[18] This book attempts to recast a larger narrative of childhood, but we should begin with a discussion of the tensions within the mainline assumptions of the field. This can be aided by returning to the Wickberg's uncomforting door and his critique of social history.

Historians of childhood have been better at organizing a field of study, than creating meaningful debate within it. For starters, it seems to me we have smoothed-over the conflict between what Wickberg calls read-ing texts as "registers of experience", and examining them for "patterns of meaning".[19] The gap between the two positions was implicit in our debates over using the term "children" or "childhood" within various organizational efforts. We split the difference and created a *Society for the History of Children and Youth* with a publication named the *Journal of Childhood and Youth*. This may seem unimportant, but "childhood" speaks to patterns of meaning; "children" lends itself to the experiences of persons. The significance becomes apparent when you compare Nicholas Orme's treatment of Pieter Brueghel's late sixteenth-century *Khinderspill* (*Children's Games*) as a record of activity and Sandra Hindman's argument

DOI: 10.1057/9781137364791

that the painting's visual structure follows the motif of the *Ages of Man*.[20] For Orme, the painting serves as a catalogue of games and proof that adults recognized that the children were playing them. It was a window upon experience. For Hindman, *Khinderspill* was produced as part of a larger discursive structure that linked childhood with human folly, and advanced the proposition that sacramental rites (such as marriage) could never tame the outrageous fortune that governed the material world. The heart of the difference between Orme and Hindman lay with divergent ways of reading evidence, and it seems to me that Hindman's reading is far more persuasive and interesting.

Reading for discourse demands more than simply stating that a category is a social construction, because it is an attempt to identify the structures of thought and practice that made a set of statements or a mode of representation possible, sometimes predictable. Discursive analysis does not reject a material world, it only rejects the idea that we have an unmediated access to it. Attempts to reconstruct historical patterns of activity, conditions, and the organization of space, time and bodies are often valuable for those interested in the structure of perception, feeling and thought.[21] Yet, a discursive approach avoids the positivist error of reading as if representations signify things or experiences, rather than ideas.[22] No text (no sign or numeral or icon or arrangement) has the power to "open doors onto the experience and imagination of children" or anyone else for that matter – if by this one imagines that we can get around the mediating power of discourse and expose an actual or essential or experiential reality.[23]

Reading for patterns of meaning (or discourse) demands an honest objection to the warning voiced by Peter Stearns against "adult sources", and rejects a quest for "sources less tainted by adulthood".[24] Setting aside forgeries, sources simply cannot be tainted in this way. They can only be misinterpreted or mistranslated. When one reads for discourse, or for modes of perception and feeling, key elements of modern "common sense" begin to fail. One cannot get *words from the horse's mouth* – from experience. Authorial intent and opinion (purportedly "biased" by individual psychological experiences and/or political-economic interests) are no longer as important as identifying the discursive structures with which all speakers in a linguistic community must contend.[25] Drawing a strong cultural divide between the generations (who – in fact – do speak the same language) comes under question. It becomes harder to imagine that a history of *children* (defined as "how children experienced" their

DOI: 10.1057/9781137364791

own lives) can be pursued as if this were free from prevailing moralities and epistemological assumptions – that is free from the discourses of childhood. The structures of *childhood* are not mere "opinions held by adults" about children. They frame the thoughts and feelings that come to bare upon both children and adults. From this perspective, Stearns' advice to read around or through the very material of analysis (representations themselves) in order to construct global evolutionary theory of humanity through a history of children seems misguided.[26]

To be sure, texts (including artefacts) produced by children and youths, or ones describing them closely, or items regularly used by them have a special evidentiary value. But this is not because they provide access to an authentic, pre-discursive experience. They offer ways to consider the layered, shared, negotiated aspects of discourse that we might otherwise misconstrue, oversimplify, or read past.[27] Refusing to read texts as means to unmediated experience does not deny children's ability to act, and it does not deny cultural diversity or conflict. It encourages us to imagine conflict, tension, paradox, negotiation, consensus, ambiguity, indeterminacy, and difference as dynamics within structures of thought and rituals of representation.[28] For historians, primary alternatives to discursive analysis are grounded in orthodox readings of Marx and Freud, and would have us position ideas as tools of agency and power. These alternatives conceptualize power and desire as external to discourse, operating in a vacuous space between interested groups or within the unconscious minds of individuals.[29]

The worst consequence of turning texts into the tools of agents would be thinking about ideas as nothing but instruments of power.[30] Childhood might be imagined to be nothing more than "adultism" – an ideology constructed by adults to keep children down.[31] Fortunately this seems rare. Most work giving a priority to children's competent agency avoids treating dominant discourses of childhood as a form of "false consciousness" or "repressed" drives. What we typically get from histories that seek children's agency is not a condemnation of dominant ideas about children, but a romance of the individual. Take David Nasaw's *Children of the City* (1985), a study that approached children "as sentient, intentional beings desirous and capable (within limits) of acting on and within their social environments".[32] We hear an echo of Marx's early respect for human agency limited by context: "Men make their own history, but they do not make it just as they please... [or] under circumstances chosen by themselves."[33] Pursuing this maxim, Nasaw brought to

DOI: 10.1057/9781137364791

life the spirit of liberal individualism in American urban childhood. For all its persuasive power, however, *Children of the City* lacked an appropriate degree of critical reflection upon its sources. It was heavily indebted to memoirs of successful Americans, at points seeming to confirm Horatio Alger's faith in the self-made man. Did Nasaw capture the experiences of children as competent agents within a specific context, or only reiterate a historically situated discourse of childhood and freedom – a body of thought that has fostered America's most stinging paradoxes?

The problems with the maxim that children are social actors cannot be finessed by following Stearn's call to avoid adult contamination of texts, because it is just as easy to uncritically read a text produced or used by children themselves. The search for children's agency and the attempt to recreate the experience of the city, itself, fostered Nasaw's blindness to the discursive structures that framed his sources. Who can gainsay what comes from the horse's mouth? Reading texts as records of experience, as if we could open doors to the mind's of individuals, limits our ability to do much with Karen Sánchez-Eppler's pointed observation that, "[e]ven for the child, the fact that childhood is lived does not prevent it from being idealized, a thing of imagination and memory."[34] When we set ourselves the task of finding agency, or positioning the subaltern as *heroes of their own lives*, to borrow Linda Gordon's terms, we pre-figure our analyses by the language of liberal individualism. It becomes very difficult to think outside the dualism between free participation and a negative, prohibitive view of power. One cannot simultaneously search for the competent individual and critically examine it as a product of power-knowledge relations.[35]

The double-meaning of *history* on Wickberg's door exposes the heart of his critical mode, because it troubles the precarious boundary between the past as a thing and our writing about it. This boundary has been challenged whenever we consider the tension between reading for discourse and reading for experience, or recognize the impossibility of searching for the competent agentive child in the records of the past, if we wish to grasp from where that image of childhood comes. Yet these two points of discomfort are more familiar to historians of childhood, than a third: the possibility that modernity itself has produced *age as a category of analysis* and fostered our propensity to see people as members of *groups within a population*. Consider an analogy. Doing the history of childhood because age is an important category of analysis seems to me like doing women's history because women are the moral pillars of the

DOI: 10.1057/9781137364791

republic. This brings us to my second claim: our capacity to unpack the untidy overlapping space between the dominant contemporary assumptions about childhood, and our larger historical inquiry into it has been immobilized by a decades-long, ill-conceived response to Ariès' 1962 landmark *Centuries of Childhood*.[36]

Many historians have expressed frustration with *Centuries of Childhood*, but for very different reasons. For Stearns, childhood and family history following Ariès (including DeMause, Stone and Shorter) was a "false-start", because it was shown to be wrong by later studies. On the contrary, it seems to me that Ariès' harshest critics have repeated his most significant mistake – his failure to read texts on their own terms.[37] Linda Pollack's *Forgotten Children* (1983) led the assault upon *Centuries* by surveying an impressively large set of diaries, mostly from the seventeenth and eighteenth centuries.[38] Unfortunately, the rise of introspective record keeping itself (the production of diaries by the gentry) does not enter the horizon of Pollack's inquiry.[39] The diaries were read to collapse the space between past and present, as windows upon experience, and to show that parents loved their children and knew they needed special care. Early-modern parents, she claimed, viewed their children as "developing organisms", even though this way of speaking and the concepts it entails are uncommon before the twentieth century. Families are said to have something closer than "formal" relationships, because we can find notes that fathers took their children fishing. The theme song from *The Andy Griffith Show* seems to be playing in the background of Pollack's reading.[40]

Contemporary concepts can not be divorced from the historical imagination, but the power of current assumptions about children should concern us. Take Barbara Hanawalt's stipulation that "a historian's task is to find out how society at the time perceived these *stages of life* and how it defined them, rather than simply accepting a present-day definition." It does not seem to have occurred to Hanawalt that the very idea that life is divided into something called "stages" is an element of modern developmental notions. Hanawalt found what she was looking for when she concluded that the, "most basic question for investigating *stages of life* in any people, in any period of history, is nurture versus nature: Is culture or biology more important? I have argued... that biology plays a very basic role in shaping the cultural parameters of childhood."[41] Once framed in the language of stage theories, Hanawalt's reading of documents was pre-figured by the tension between biological development and childhood socialization, even

DOI: 10.1057/9781137364791

though the contemporary nature-nurture debate is foreign to the structure of medieval thought. The potential for interpretative disaster when we read modern discourses of childhood into medieval texts was made devastatingly clear by James Schultz's 2004 attack upon Nicholas Orme's *Medieval Children*. Schultz began by noting that the book was heavily weighted with examples from the Renaissance and the Reformation recast as medieval. Even when Orme "does have [appropriate] evidence, his certainty that medieval children were 'ourselves' leads him to misread it".[42]

The primary consequence of the attack upon *Centuries* from Pollack, Hanawalt, Orme and others has been to neutralize the book's primary virtue – making childhood historically significant to a wide audience of scholars. Their transcendent picture of childhood erodes the most compelling reason for pursuing the field. Why write something called the history of childhood, if childhood is not historical? Inadvertently – their response to *Centuries*, and more generally their attack on the Annales School, logically entails leaving childhood to be studied under ahistorical research programmes. Those who are interested in the historicity of childhood over the *longue durée* will have to offer an alternative reading of Ariès.

Colin Heywood has voiced a dissatisfaction with the response to *Centuries*. He observed that Albrecht Classen's grand 2005 proclamation of a "paradigm shift" in the history of childhood had "rather disappointingly" offered the conclusion that "children were well regarded in the Middle Ages and fully recognized as children, that is not as young adults".[43] Perhaps, Heywood was too polite to say the obvious: Classen's conclusions simply do not justify childhood as an historically significant field for research. A similar problem appears in Louise Wilkinson introduction to an important 2010 collection. She denounces Ariès, defends Pollack's transcendent view of parental affection, and reiterates Hanawalt's biological determinism. Interestingly enough, she advanced a very different perspective on the sexual hierarchy of the Middle Ages; it was "imposed" by historically grounded arrangements.[44] The inconvenient question has to be asked again: if gender is historical and political, and age is neither, is the history of childhood an antiquarian endeavour? Are we providing background information for the "real" childhood researchers in the sciences of the body and the professionals running institutions of discipline?

Though exceedingly charitable, Heywood's review of the literature makes it plain that historians should seek a new "way forward" beyond

DOI: 10.1057/9781137364791

the old debate over *Centuries*. Following the mainline assumptions, he argued that historians should "assume that social groups have some scope for constructing their own model of childhood, which will affect the experience of young people growing up under its influence". Childhood is "neither a natural nor universal feature of human groups".[45] I agree with moving in this direction, but I do not think Heywood goes far enough. As this book will argue, "experience" and (especially) the idea of "human groups" must be part of the list of ideas requiring a historical lens if we are interested in understanding childhood as a structure of thought.

Merridee Bailey puts herself on the horns of this problem (encountered by Hanawalt and Heywood) when she stipulates that childhood "represents more than a chronological age or a physical form; it is a time of instruction and learning, when relationships and abilities are developed and identity is created". For Bailey, *identity*, *development* and *ability* (and more generally *socialization*) served as a transhistorical grounding for reading early-modern courtesy books, "in relation to the social and economic desires of these groups".[46] An alternative approach would be to situate the rise of courtesy literature as a genre shift that paved the way for a modern pre-occupation with ordinary children's education. Quentin Skinner, Charles Taylor and Stephan Greenblatt have provided different ways for reading Renaissance humanism as the foundation for a distinctly modern worldview, but incorporating their work into a history of childhood would require a history of ideas, sentiments or discourse that departs from the assumptions of a history of persons and experiences.[47]

When we write the history of childhood as a story of individuals negotiating their identities as members of groups – assigning a transhistorical designation to what Taylor called the "buffered self" (whether we imagine children as persons experiencing conditioning, development, authenticity or exercising agency) – we have enclosed our efforts within the discursive structure of modernity.[48] This may sharpen our ability to find points of continuity between past and present and enable us to tell a story of progress or decline, but it will blind us to the foreignness of the distant past and the deep structure of childhood itself. It seems to me that a transhistorical assumption of modern concepts of human development operate when historians read hagiographic stories to show an "awareness of... a normal child's existence". It is present when the *ages of man* is referred to as evidence of awareness of the "phase[s] of life", appearing

DOI: 10.1057/9781137364791

continuously from antiquity to the early-modern era.[49] Historians cross-reference documents to produce the ages of individuals where the texts themselves do not render this data systematically. Marriage becomes a pathway to "social adulthood", or "economic adulthood". Religious confirmation becomes a rite of "religious adulthood".[50] Masters become "employers"; servants are renamed "employees".[51] Didactic texts defining an etiquette of service, deference and obligation are positioned as child-rearing advice to parents, or self-help books for youths. We may have more information about the history of childhood than ever before, but these are the same types of interpretive shortcomings found in *Centuries of Childhood* a half-century ago.

Paula Fass has added her persuasive voice to the call for the field to move beyond *Centuries of Childhood*. She asks whether, "we now have a story good enough to replace [Ariès]", and will it redirect the "attention" that continues to be directed at his book? Her answer is to cast the story of childhood more clearly than ever as part of the "aspiring universalism" of humanity. She says this aspiration was grounded in ancient traditions, but has been renewed by the processes of globalization. For Fass, modern childhood emerged as access to a "privileged state", a group living according to middle-class morality. Modern childhood is way of life that did not become widely available until the nineteenth century when it was "adopted by various institutions that enshrined" it as part of the purpose of the modern state. During the last two centuries, childhood started to break-through race, class, gender and other boundaries; it became a "paradigm" of humanitarianism "that spread beyond the developed West to exercise increasing influence on the nature of childhood images and children's experiences throughout the globe". Fass' childhood is the key to modern progress toward human dignity and meaningful freedom.[52]

At the risk of reducing her arguments to bare essentials, Fass inverts Ariès. The fact that she is operating in a similar mode (in reverse) might explain why she tends to avoid repeating certain well-worn, half-truths about *Centuries*.[53] The typical distortion wrongly lumps Ariès with DeMause, Shorter and Stone, and reduces *Centuries* to the idea that childhood didn't exist in the Middle Ages, that children were little adults prior to modernity, or that high mortality created emotional distance.[54] In fact, the main argument of *Centuries* depicted the moralizing school and private family as remaking childhood as a site for social discipline.[55] It is worth quoting Ariès' conclusion at length:

We have seen however, until the eighteenth-century, [early-modern ideas about childhood, family privacy, and the school] failed to destroy the old sociability... [but in time] it spread to all classes and imposed itself tyrannically on people's consciousness. The evolution of the last few centuries has often been presented as the triumph of individualism over social constraints... where is the individualism in these modern lives, in which all the energy of the couple is directed to serving the interests of a deliberately restricted posterity? Was there not greater individualism in the gay indifference of the prolific fathers of the ancien regime?[56]

We might say that *Centuries* put a twentieth-century twist upon the troubled relationship that romantics, since Rousseau, have had with bourgeois self-control. If this reading is correct, it would be important to recognize that within the precise historical era where Ariès thought our manhood (authentic freedom) was lost, Fass locates the triumph of our humanity (the conditions for decency) in the care of children. It seems to me that the difference between Ariès and Fass plays with a well-established point of opposition upon the landscape of modern childhood.[57] This is not offered to delegitimate their competing narratives. But, it does suggest that adhering too closely to either one may obscure our ability to investigate structures of childhood that preceded the modern discourses of universal liberation (or its betrayal).

This book is the first part of a larger attempt to delineate the deep historical structure of childhood. It questions some of the mainline assumptions in the history of childhood and departs from the narratives offered by Ariès, Stone, deMause, Stearns and Fass. The remainder of this introduction will outline my approach and summarize the substantive argument of the book. Let me begin by making some of the premises of my analysis explicit.

1   Discourse is not an opinion, a conversation, or a particular
    representation. It is not the opposite of practice. Discourses
    are bodies of thought, rituals of inscription that allow any
    utterance, any practice, any representation to operate and make
    sense. Speaking of discursive structure does not preclude the
    acknowledgement that ambiguity, indeterminacy, conflict (and
    even happenstance) are important parts of human history, but it
    does set a goal of trying to find patterns of sentiment: thought and
    feeling.
2   If we want to better understand the deep structure of childhood
    we have to be willing to work over vast periods of time. We cannot

DOI: 10.1057/9781137364791

brush quickly over the daunting scope of medieval history, or avoid the learned, detailed work that one finds in medieval studies. We should take the Middle Ages seriously, and try to understand them on their own terms. Writing a history since 1500 will not do, if we ultimately wish to understand the distinctive features of modernity.

3 This study provides an anatomy of the vocabulary of childhood in Anglo-Saxon and Middle English as part of an attempt to unpack the roots of early-modern English. Using philology as a skeletal structure, I have synthesized an interdisciplinary spectrum of research, including economic, religious, political and legal history, art history, historical sociology, literature, philosophy, and theology. The goal has been to gain a coherent view of the discursive structure of childhood in English before modernity. Our primary boundaries are linguistic (English), rather than geographic. However, the ontological issues of sections four and five required an examination of European history on a wider scope and call us back to the ancients.

4 As a whole, this book provides an outline (not a thick description) of the dominant discourse of childhood from the Christianization of the Anglo-Saxons in the seventh-century into early-modern English culture. The book argues that master-servant relations structured the meanings of childhood for at least a millennium. Childhood was embedded in master-servant relations, but this was something more than a hierarchy of labour. The master-servant sense of being in time – or *age* – was an extension of, was justified by, and experienced through a double-sense of time and space foreign to the modern mind. Being in time was lived as a correspondence between ordinary secular or linear existence and eternal, cosmic order, or the essence of things.

To speak of "master-servant" childhood is not to say that children were mistreated or despised as a rule. What follows should make it clear that it is nonsense to say children were viewed as "little adults", and that there is scant evidence of an "emotional distance" in family ideals and relations during the Middle Ages. Locating childhood within the dynamics of master-servant discourse provides a much more interesting way to approach the strange gap between medieval and modern sensibilities about age, generations, and what it is to be and to become human.

The first chapter of the book shows that the language of medieval family life and marriage united the ideas of male possession of land

DOI: 10.1057/9781137364791

with master-servant relations of labour and through paternal patterns of inheritance. The Middle English terms for males, and some of their Anglo-Saxon counterparts, distinguished men by property status; whereas the most common words for females across the entire medieval period, positioned them in terms of sexual experience, sexual availability, marital status and motherhood. Aligned around land, sex and lineage, this vocabulary was insensitive to the age of persons, and unsuited to express the idea of a romantic conjugal unit, or the modern family.

The growing intervention of the Church into matters of marriage and family, well-established by the thirteenth century, advanced patriarchal ways of family life. There exists an hint of continuity with modern gender politics here, but the language of kinship in medieval England tied together material property, householding, marriage and labour relations in ways that are foreign to the contemporary mind. For one, neither the land nor the household could be easily quantified or alienated from personhood prior to the sixteenth century. The very terms of family and marriage implied a positive cultural association between the possession of land and the varieties of household belonging. A medieval sense of ownership or household bonds did not follow the modern dualism between mere market price and the priceless relations of a loving family.

Chapter 2 begins with the observation that patriarchal households could not operate solely through the structures of marriage, sex and land ownership. They required a wider arrangement of labour which defined generational relations, and what it meant to be a young person. The institution of apprenticeship will be examined to capture the significance of household servitude for the meaning of boyhood in England during the late-medieval and early-modern eras. Many of the surviving words (*boy, lad, girl, maid*) still carry a sense of service, but in Middle English and Anglo-Saxon these terms' precursors denoted a position of servitude first, sometimes without any connotation of age, and in a few instances, without gender specificity. In the larger medieval and early modern cultural imagination, female attendants or maids were not the conceptual opposites of apprentices, students or other serving boys. All these ordinary subject positions for males and females stood in distinction to the "vagabond" – an unbound, propertyless person living outside household authority and therefore outside the law itself. By contrast, ordinary twentieth-century youths ("the teenagers") are positioned in opposition to both relations of obedience and labour.

DOI: 10.1057/9781137364791

Chapter 3 will shift our focus from the household toward an examination of those words most directly tied to the concept of a "child". Indeed, these emerged from a different matrix: coming down from words for the womb and the idea of pregnancy. At the base of this complex of words, there was a conceptual split between bodily growth and lineal descent. The former group expressed worldly existence and change, and the other carried a sense of transcendent essence. This generative tension (existence-essence) was useful well into the early-modern period, as the terms of childhood often signified human folly, chaos and mortality, while they also served to denote the human capacity to discern the order of the cosmos, or to be adopted into communion with God. At the risk oversimplification, one might say that the popular contemporary belief has the medieval world backwards: this was not a world without childhood, it was a world without adulthood. The figure of the mature, competent individual was not central to the culture. Prior to the sixteenth century, English entirely lacked terminology fit for a discourse of either developmental socialization, or the autonomous romantic subject. The medieval conceptualization of childhood was organized around a sense of age and generations with which moderns are unfamiliar.

The semantic shifts between medieval and modern vocabularies of households (land-sex-marriage) and servitude (boy-youth-servant) are relatively straight-forward. The modern discourse of marriage and sex has been cut away from the terms of household production and landed inheritance; while the ideas associated with youth have been separated from servitude under the modern employee-employer relationship. The narrative of a rise of market society (or capitalism) provides a useful way of explaining both these transformations. The same cannot be said for the conceptualization of childhood as it relates directly to the ideas associated with age, time, being, generation and origins. To confront this more subtle ontological shift, the final two chapters of the book consider the historical narrative of childhood beyond medieval England.

Chapter 4 begins by summarizing some of the compelling evidence that Europeans since antiquity have been concerned with the care of children. There is a deep, if ambiguous, reservoir of emotion entangled with reproduction and childcare in European cultural history. Yet, the ancient way of confronting the precariousness of our existence – the mortality of being in time – followed a logic of correspondence that has increasingly lost its force since the sixteenth century. We find this older search for resemblance and similitude operating within numerology,

DOI: 10.1057/9781137364791

astrology, biblical hermeneutics and Aristotelian thought. It required a double-sense that ordinary time as experienced on earth was always already contingent upon eternal order, a time out of mind, a time of origins, or Providence. Here we introduce the Greek discussion of *paideia*, the Christian concept of *imago Dei*, and the ubiquitous representational device called *The Ages of Man* to show that the medieval cosmos was continuous and animated (as opposed to an atomistic and Epicurean). Ordinary things could be read for the revelation of a divine structure. In English, the precursors to *kind, nature, generation*, and other words helped late-medieval, early-modern persons speak of an unchanging essence ordering a precarious world. There was no mechanistic, internal search for cause and specific difference: few devices of hierarchical observation and no language of normalizing judgment. Being in time was a parallel, cyclical and reversible relationship between existence and essence.

The concluding section starts with a discussion of the limits of representation as they relate to the semantic history of childhood. The verb *to be* has no meaning because it serves to make all propositions, all statements of truth possible. The limits of representation are found at the impossibility of identifying the meaning of *to be*. This uncertainty and instability is the most general and the oldest problem of knowledge about being human. Its special relationship to childhood has not been widely acknowledged. As in many languages, the terms of childhood in English are grounded in the verb *to be* through the concept of *age* or being in time, and in the semantic history of the terms for womb, pregnancy and origins. The significance of this semantic history has been obscured by the dominant discourses of modernity, established under the human sciences since the seventeenth century, whereby childhood became an object of study, a means around the limits of representation – around language itself.

Our ability to assess historical shifts in the linguistic structure of childhood are not entirely lost with the impenetrability of the verb *to be*. What follows will outline a vocabulary that situated childhood within the patriarchal household, inseparable from the practices of servitude. More subtly, the terms of master-servant childhood, age and generations will be shown to have followed a logic of correspondence and the ancient existence-essence distinction that was incommensurate with modernity's Epicurean revival. The book will conclude with a series of literary comparisons designed to emphasize the medieval-modern distinction by drawing on texts as seemingly unrelated as those from the *Feast of*

DOI: 10.1057/9781137364791

the Holy Innocents with the modern novel *Moby Dick*; and the emancipation narratives of medieval saints as contrasted with those of American slaves.

Grasping the terms of master-servant relations as a coherent whole allows us to illuminate the structures of thought that separate medieval childhood from the present. The medieval sense of being and becoming was defined by a continuous, animated cosmos. Master-servant childhood was part of a relational, external search for correspondence and resemblance, rather than a mechanistic, internal search for cause and specific difference. Time existed as a parallel, cyclical and reversible arrangement of existence and essence, rather according to measurable units of linear development. The modern world's normalizing terms of childhood allow contemporary English-speakers to imagine that the essence of being human might be achieved by becoming fully, completely, finally – an adult. No such destination of developmental socialization governed the medieval sense of the self. For a millennium of English history, childhood presented a very different opportunity: a hermeneutic for grasping the great chain of being. How and why the terms of master-servant childhood came unraveled between 1500 and 1800 is a topic for ongoing study.

Notes

1   Lloyd deMause, *The History of Childhood* (New York, NY: Harper & Row, 1974): 1.
2   See the charts in Jack H. Hexter, "Fernand Braudel and the Monde Braudellien...," *The Journal of Modern History* vol. 44, no. 4 (December 1972): 480–539.
3   See especially Daniel Wickberg, "Intellectual History vs. the Social History of Intellectuals," *Rethinking History* vol. 5, no. 3 (2001): 383–395; and "What is the History of Sensibilities: On Cultural Histories, Old and New," *American Historical Review* vol. 112, no. 3 (June 2007): 661–684. Between these two essays, the phrase "the cultural history of representation" replaced "the social history of intellectuals", and the "history of sensibilities", replaced "intellectual history". The new labels advanced a more nuanced picture of the battle between historical sociology and the history of ideas, particularly for the history of mentality or emotion. The shift also may have enhanced the reception that Wickberg's arguments received among historians. But the two articles share the same internal

DOI: 10.1057/9781137364791

logic and epistemological commitments, which informed his 1998 book *The Sense of Humor*. See the exchange with Barbara Rosenwein in the *American Historical Review* vol. 112, no. 4 (October 2007): 1313–1315. Also see, Daniel Wickberg, "Homophobia: On the Cultural History of an Idea," *Critical Inquiry* 27 (Autumn 2000): 42–57; "Heterosexual White Male: Some Recent Inversions in American Cultural History," *The Journal of American History* vol. 92, no. 1 (June 2005): 136–157; "The Current State of Intellectual History: A Forum," *Historically Speaking* vol. 10, no. 4 (September 2009): 14–24; "Questioning the Assumptions of Academic History: a Forum," *Historically Speaking* vol. 12, no 1. (January 2011): 10–20.

4   On socialization and symbolic interaction see works by Margaret Mead, George Herbert Mead, Charles Horton Cooley, Erik Erikson, Erving Goffman, and Herbert Blumer; on modernization and generational relations see works by Willard Waller, August Hollingshead, Talcott Parsons, Shmuel N. Eisenstadt, James S. Coleman, David Riesman, Paul Goodman, and Kenneth Keniston. Historians began taking childhood, youth and generations more seriously from the late 1950s in an effort to understand the transmission of culture, political change or social control. See important works by Philippe Ariès, Oscar Handlin, Bernard Bailyn, Bernard Wishy, John Demos, Philip Greven, Lawrence Stone, Edward Shorter, Robert Bremner, Anthony Platt, John Gillis, Paula Fass, Joseph Kett, Tamara Hareven, Joseph Hawes, Ray Hiner, Michael Haines, and many others. At the same moment, the history of American education became something more than a project of professionalization; see especially the works by Lawrence Cremin, David Tyack, Stanley K. Schultz, or Joel Spring among others.

5   In education and social mobility, see Paul Willis, *Learning to Labor: how Working Class Kids Get Working Class Jobs* (New York, NY: Columbia University Press, 1977); Reed Ueda, *Avenues to Adulthood: The Origins of the High School and Social Mobility in An American Suburb* (New York: Cambridge University Press, 1987); Paula Fass, *Outside In: Minorities and the Transformation of American Education* (New York, NY: Oxford University Press, 1989); Ileen DeVault, *Sons and Daughters of Labor: Class and Clerical Work in Turn-of-the-Century Pittsburgh* (Ithaca, NY: Cornell University Press, 1990). A focus on group contest and the identification process framed work more generally; see Linda Gordon, *The Great Arizona Orphan Abduction* (Cambridge, MA: Harvard University Press, 1999); Steven Mintz, *Huck's Raft: A History of American* (Cambridge, MA: The Belknap Press of Harvard University Press, 2005); Cynthia R. Comacchio *The Dominion of Youth: Adolescence and the Making of Modern Canada, 1902–1950* (Waterloo, ON: Wilfrid Laurier University, 2006).

6   Steven Scholssman and Stephanie Wallach, "The Crime of Precocious Sexuality: Female Juvenile Delinquency in the Progressive Era," *Harvard*

DOI: 10.1057/9781137364791

Educational Review vol. 48, no. 1 (Spring 1978): 65–94; Viviana A. Zelizer, *Pricing the Priceless Child: The Changing Social Value of Children* (New York, NY: Basic Books, 1985); Howard P. Chudacoff, *How Old Are You?: Age Consciousness in American Culture* (Princeton, NJ: Princeton University Press, 1989); Paula Fass, *Kidnapped: Child Abduction in America* (New York, NY: Oxford University Press, 1997); Philip Jenkins, *Moral Panic: Changing Concepts of the Child Molester in Modern America* (New Haven, CT: Yale University Press, 1998). See the forums on "The Crime of Precocious Sexuality," and *Pricing the Priceless Child* in the *Journal of the History of Childhood and Youth* vol. 2, no 1 (Winter 2009), and vol. 5, no. 3 (Fall 2012), respectively.

7 John Springhall, *Coming of Age: Adolescence in Britain, 1860–1960* (Dublin: Gill and Macmillan, 1986); William Graebner, *Coming of Age in Buffalo: Youth and Authority in the Postwar Era* (Philadelphia, PA: Temple University Press, 1990); Kriste Lindenmeyer, *The Greatest Generation Grows Up: American Childhood in the 1930s* (Chicago, IL: Ivan R. Dee, 2005); Melissa R. Klapper, *Jewish Girls Coming of Age, 1860–1920* (New York, NY: New York University Press, 2007); Emma E. Werner, *In Pursuit of Liberty: Coming of Age in the American Revolution* (Washington, DC: Potomac Books, 2009).

8 Harry Hendrick, "The Child as a Social Actor in Historical Sources: Problems of Identification and Interpretation," in *Research with Children: Perspectives and Practices* edited by Pia Christensen and Allison James (London, UK: Falmer Press, 2000): 36.

9 Resistance to orthodox views of developmental socialization came to the fore during the 1970s and 1980s from social and psychological scientists as varied as Myra Bluebond-Langner, Robert Coles, Valerie Walkerdine, Nikolas Rose, and John Morss. The challenge continued with efforts by Alan Prout, Allison James, Chris Jenks, Jens Qvortrup, Nick Lee, Martin Woodhead, and many others; in particular see Erica Burman, *Deconstructing Developmental Psychology* (New York, NY: Routledge, 1994); Gareth B. Matthews, *The Philosophy of Childhood* (Cambridge, MA: Harvard University Press, 1996); William A. Corsaro, *The Sociology of Childhood* (Thousand Oaks, CA: Pine Forge Press, 1997); Tobias Hecht's *At Home in the Street: Street Children of Northeast Brazil* (Cambridge, UK: Press Synicate of the University of Cambridge, 1998); Manfred Liebel, *A Will of Their Own: Cross-Cultural Perspectives on Working Children* (New York, NY: Zed Books, 2004); Allison J. Pugh, *Longing and Belonging: Parents, Children, and Consumer Culture* (Berkeley, CA: University of California Press, 2009).

10 Ian Hacking, *The Social Construction of What?* (Cambridge, MA: Harvard University Press, 1999). The emphasis on children as a social actors/ childhood as socially constructed remains a predominant theme. See Mary Niall Mitchell, "Children and Childhood," *The William and Mary Quarterly* vol. 69, no. 1 (January 2011): 173–177.

DOI: 10.1057/9781137364791

11 For attempts to integrate science and history see John Modell, *Into One's Own: From Youth to Adulthood in the United States, 1920–1975* (Berkeley, CA: University of California Press, 1989); Glen H. Elder, John Modell and Ross D. Parke (eds) *Children in Time and Place: Developmental and Historical Insights* (New York, NY: Cambridge University Press, 1993); Willem Koops and Michael Zuckerman (eds), *Beyond the Century of the Child: Cultural History and Developmental Psychology* (Philadelphia, PA: University of Pennsylvania, 2003); Anthony Volk, "The Evolution of Childhood," *The Journal of the History of Childhood and Youth* vol. 4, no. 3 (Fall 2011): 470–494. Among medievalists, those who accept the assumptions of developmental science include Barbara Hanawalt, Shulamith Shahar, Sally Crawford and Nicolas Orme; all cited below.

12 Joan Jacobs Brumberg, *Fasting Girls: The History of Anorexia Nervosa* (Cambridge, MA: Harvard University Press, 1988); Nikolas Rose, *Governing the Soul: The Shaping of the Private Self,* org. publ. 1989 (New York, NY: Free Association Books, 1999): 123–216; Mona Gleason, *Normalizing the Ideal: Psychology, Schooling, and the Family in Postwar Canada* (Toronto, ON: University of Toronto Press, 1999); Crista Deluzio, *Female Adolescence in American Scientific Thought, 1830–1930* (Baltimore, MD: Johns Hopkins University Press, 2007); Andre Turmel, *A Historical Sociology of Childhood: Developmental Thinking, Categorization, and Graphic Visualization* (Cambridge, UK: Cambridge University Press, 2008); Andrew F. Jones, *Developmental Fairy Tales: Evolutionary Thinking and Modern Chinese Culture* (Cambridge, MA: Harvard University Press, 2011).

13 Judith Plotz, *Romanticism and the Vocation of Childhood* (New York, NY: Palgrave Macmillan, 2001); Daniel T. Cook, *The Commodification of Childhood: The Children's Clothing Industry and the Rise of the Child Consumer* (Durham, NC: Duke University Press, 2004); Gary S. Cross, *The Cute and the Cool: Wondrous Innocence and Modern American Children's Culture* (New York, NY: Oxford University Press, 2004); Karen Sánchez-Eppler *Dependent States: The Child's Part in Nineteenth-Century American Culture* (Chicago: University Press, 2005); Howard Chudacoff, *Children at Play: An American History* (New York, NY: New York University Press, 2007); Loren Lerner (ed.), *Depicting Canada's Children* (Waterloo, ON: Wilfrid Laurier University Press, 2009); Anja Muller (ed.), *Fashioning Childhood in the Eighteenth-Century: Age and Identity* (Burlington, VT: Ashgate, 2006); Anja Muller, *Framing Childhood in Eighteenth-Century English Periodicals and Prints, 1689–1789* (Burlington, VT: Ashgate, 2009); Karen Sánchez-Eppler, "Marks of Possession: Methods for an Impossible Subject," *Publications of the Modern Language Association of America* vol. 126, no. 1 (January 2011): 151–159.

14 The studies that cross the domains of disability, policy, and childhood history are numerous. See recent works such as Chris F. Goodey, *A History*

DOI: 10.1057/9781137364791

of Intelligence and "Intellectual Disability": The Shaping of Psychology in Early Modern Europe (Burlington, VT: Ashgate Publishing Company, 2011); Gil Eyal et al., *The Autism Matrix: The Social Origins of the Autism Epidemic* (Cambridge, UK: Polity Press, 2010); Steven Noll and James W. Trent, Jr. (eds), *Mental Retardation in America: A Historical Reader* (New York, NY: New York University Press, 2004).

15 Three key organizational efforts were: 1) The establishment of *H-Childhood* under *H-Net* in 1998; 2) The founding of *The Society for the History of Children and Youth* in 2001; 3) The successful launching of *The Journal of the History of Childhood and Youth* in 2008.

16 Martha Saxton, "Introduction," *The Journal of the History of Childhood and Youth* vol. 1, no. 1 (Winter 2008): 1–3. Emphasis added. See the forum, "Age as a Category of Historical Analysis" in the same issue.

17 Patrick J. Ryan, "How New is the 'New' Social Studies of Childhood? The Myth of a Paradigm Shift," *Journal of Interdisciplinary History* vol. 38, no. 4 (Spring 2008): 553–576.

18 Philippe Ariès, *Centuries of Childhood – A Social History of Family Life* trans. Robert Baldick (New York, NY: Vintage Books, 1962).

19 Wickberg, "Intellectual History vs. the Social History of Intellectuals," 384; "What is the History of Sensibilities," 671.

20 Nicholas Orme, *Medieval Children* (New Haven, CN: Yale University Press, 2001): 166–167; Sandra Hindman, "Pieter Bruegel's Children's Games, Folly, and Chance," *The Art Bulletin* vol. 63, no. 3 (September 1981): 447–475.

21 On material culture in Marta Gutman and Ning de Coninck-Smith (eds), *Designing Modern Childhoods: History, Space, and the Material Culture of Childhood* (New Brunswick, NJ: Rutgers University Press, 2008); Karin Calvert, *Children of the House: The Material Culture of Early Childhood, 1600–1900* (Boston: Northeastern University Press, 1992).

22 See Joan W. Scott, "The Evidence of Experience," *Critical Inquiry* vol. 17 (1991): 773–797.

23 There are various ways to take this approach. See Michel Foucault, *The Essential Foucault: Selections from the Essential Works of Foucault, 1954–1984* (New York, NY: New Press, 2003): 377–391; Stanley Fish, *The Stanley Fish Reader* edited by H. Aram Veeser (Malden, MA: Blackwell Publishers, 1999); Clifford Geertz, *Local Knowledge: Further Essays in Interpretive Anthropology* (New York, NY: Basic Books, 1983).

24 Peter Stearns, "Challenges in the History of Childhood," *The Journal of the History of Childhood and Youth* vol. 1, no. 1 (Winter 2008): 35–42.

25 The distinction between "objects of representation" and "modes of perception and feeling" is handled thoughtfully in Wickberg, "What is the History of Sensibilities," 661–663.

DOI: 10.1057/9781137364791

26   Peter Stearns, *Growing Up: The History of Childhood in Global Context* (Waco, TX: Baylor, 2005).

27   For an example of such as study, see Patrick J. Ryan, "'Young Rebels Flee Psychology': Individual Intelligence, Race, and Foster Children in Cleveland, Ohio between the World Wars," *Paedagogica Historica* vol. 47, no. 6 (October 2011): 767–783.

28   This is the main point of Foucault's term "power-knowledge". See Michel Foucault, *Power/Knowledge: Selected Interviews & Other Writings 1972–1977* edited by Colin Gordon (New York, NY: Pantheon Books, 1980).

29   Ironically, the two main sources of this problem are also the most important wellsprings for contemporary critiques of modern liberal conceptualizations of power: Marx's concept of *ideology* and Freud's concept of *defense mechanisms*. Valuable alternative ways to think about ideas and power were offered by Raymond Williams on hegemony and "structures of feeling" in *Marxism and Literature* (New York, NY: Oxford University Press, 1977). On Foucault's theses on power, see the sound commentary offered by Todd May, *The Philosophy of Foucault* (Montreal, QC: McGill-Queen's University Press, 2006); Dianna Taylor (ed.), *Michel Foucault: Key Concepts* (Durham, UK: Acumen, 2011).

30   Wickberg, "Intellectual History vs. the Social History of Intellectuals," 388–90.

31   This is the root flaw of deMause's reading, but it also appears in other works, such as Joseph L. Zornado, *Inventing the Child: Culture, Ideology, and the Story of Childhood* (New York, NY: Garland Publishers, 2001).

32   David Nasaw, *Children of the City – At Work and At Play* (New York, NY: Oxford University Press, 1985): 7.

33   From *The Eighteenth Brumaire of Louis Napoleon* in Jon Elster (ed.), *Karl Marx – A Reader* (Cambridge, UK: Cambridge University Press, 1986): 277.

34   Sánchez-Eppler, *Dependent*, xxvi.

35   For reading texts produced by youths without accepting liberal assumptions about agency see Patrick J. Ryan, "A Case Study in the Cultural Origins of a Superpower: Liberal Individualism, American Nationalism, and the Rise of High School Life – A Study of Cleveland's Central and East Technical High Schools, 1890–1918," *The History of Education Quarterly* vol. 45, no. 1 (Spring 2005): 66–95.

36   For thoughtful reviews of Ariès and his critics see James Schultz *The Knowledge of Childhood in the German Middle Ages, 1100–1350* (Philadelphia, PA: University of Pennsylvania Press, 1995): 1–20; Margaret L. King, "Concepts of Childhood: What We Know and Where We Might Go," *Renaissance Quarterly* vol. 60 (2007): 371–407; Jeroen J.H. Dekker and Leendert F. Groenendijk, "Philippe Ariès Discovery of Childhood after Fifty Years: the Impact of a Classic Study on Educational Research," *Oxford Review of Education* vol. 38, no 2 (April 2012): 133–147.

DOI: 10.1057/9781137364791

37 This critique of Ariès' reading was offered persuasively by Adrian Wilson, "The Infancy of the History of Childhood: An Appraisal of Philippe Ariès," *History and Theory* vol. 19, no. 2 (February 1980): 132–153.

38 Linda A. Pollack, *Forgotten Children: Parent-Child Relations from 1500–1900* (New York, NY: Cambridge University Press, 1983).

39 The issue is handled much better by Jacqueline S. Reinier, *From Virtue to Character: American Childhood, 1775–1850* (New York, NY: Twayne Publishers, 1996).

40 Pollack, *Forgotten Children*, 97–98, 100.

41 Barbara Hanawalt, *Growing Up in Medieval England: The Experience of Childhood in History* (New York, NY: Oxford University Press, 1993): 9.

42 James A. Schultz, "Nicholas Orme, *Medieval Children*," *Medievalia et Humanistica* vol. 30 (2004): 156–159.

43 Colin Heywood, "*Centuries of Childhood*: An Anniversary – and an Epitaph," *Journal of the History of Childhood and Youth* vol. 3, no. 3 (Fall 2010): 350.

44 Louise J. Wilkinson, *A Cultural History of Childhood and Family in the Middle Ages – Volume 2* (New York, NY: Berg, 2010): 1–19.

45 Heywood, "*Centuries of Childhood*," 354, 350, 347.

46 Merridee L. Bailey, *Socialising the Child in Late Medieval England*, c. 1400–1600, (Woodbridge, UK: York University Press, 2012): 1, 26.

47 Quentin Skinner, *The Foundations of Modern Political Thought* (New York, NY: Cambridge University Press, 1978); Charles Taylor, *A Secular Age* (Cambridge, MA: The Belknap Press of Harvard University Press, 2007); Stephen Greenblatt, *The Swerve: How the World Became Modern* (New York, NY: W.W. Norton & Company, 2011).

48 Taylor, *Secular Age*, 27. Also see Philip Gleason, "Identifying Identity: A Semantic History" in *The Journal of American History* vol. 69 no. 4 (March 1983): 910–931; Charles Taylor, *Sources of the Self: The Making of Modern Identity* (Cambridge, MA: Harvard University Press, 1989). For an outline of the major threads that make-up the discursive structure of modern childhood see Patrick J. Ryan, "Discursive Tensions on the Landscape of Modern Childhood," *Educare – Veteskapliga Skrifter* (2011: 2): 11–37; and my articles cited above – "'Young Rebels Flee Psychology'" and "How New is the 'New' Social Studies of Childhood?"

49 These are Heywood's summary assessments on Ronald Finucane, *The Rescue of the Innocents* (New York: St. Martin's Press, 1997); Elizabeth Sears, *The Ages of Man: Medieval Interpretations of the Life Cycle* (Princeton, NJ: Princeton University Press, 1986).

50 Stearns, *Growing Up*, 12; P.J.P. Goldberg, *Medieval England: A Social History, 1250–1550* (London: Hodder Arnold, 2004).

51 P.J.P. Goldberg, "What was a Servant?" in *Concepts and Patterns of Service in the Later Middle Ages* edited by Elizabeth Matthew and Anne Curry (Woodbridge, UK: Boydell Press, 2000): 1–20.

DOI: 10.1057/9781137364791

52   Paula Fass (ed.), *The Routledge History of Childhood in the Western World* (New
       York, NY: Routledge, 2013): 1–14. Fass has developed this line of thought
       over a number of publications. See "Children and Globalization," *The Journal
       of Social History* vol. 36, no. 4 (Summer 2003): 963–977; *Children of a New
       World: Society, Culture, and Globalization* (New York University Press, 2007);
       "The World is at Our Door: Why Historians of Children and Childhood
       should Open Up," *The Journal of the History of Childhood and Youth* vol. 1, no. 1
       (Winter 2008): 11–31.

53   A particularly egregious distortion of *Centuries* was delivered by Albrecht
       Classen, "Philippe Ariès and the Consequences: History of Childhood, Family
       Relations, and Personal Emotions, Where do We Stand Today?" in *Childhood
       in the Middle Ages and the Renaissance: The Results of a Paradigm Shift in the
       History of Mentality* (New York, NY: Walter de Gruyter, 2005): 1–65. Classen
       merged Ariès with deMause in order to claim that the *Ariès Thesis* positioned
       childhood in the "dark ages", as a time when people "badly mistreated their
       children, neglected them, or regularly spanked them brutally, if they did not
       even kill them in times of famines" (p. 23). From this position, Classen elevated
       the *Ariès Thesis* to a "paradigm", furthering something called "pastism", or
       negative attitudes toward the medieval world (p. 20).

54   Ariès, *Centuries of Childhood*, 128. Ariès most cited passage that in
       "medieval society the idea of childhood did not exist" is rarely quoted with
       the remainder of the sentence; "this is not to suggest that children were
       neglected, forsaken, or despised" (p. 128). The phrase "small adult" does
       appear on the back cover of the English translation, but I was not able to
       find it within the pages of the text. The most cited passage summarized only
       the first one-third part of the book. The section that presents it is entitled,
       "The Two Concepts of Childhood," which directs us to the idea delivered in
       the remainder of the book that a "modern" concept emerged between the
       fifteenth and the eighteenth centuries. See Roger Cox for commentary on the
       famous passage in *Shaping Childhood: Themes of Uncertainty in the History of
       Adult-Child Relationships* (New York, NY: Routledge, 1996): 1–2.

55   "The essential difference between the medieval school and the modern
       college lies in the introduction of discipline." Ariès, *Centuries of Childhood*,
       333.

56   Ariès, *Centuries of Childhood*, 406.

57   See Ryan, "Discursive Tensions on the Landscape of Modern Childhood".

DOI: 10.1057/9781137364791

1

Husbands, Wives and the Language of Patriarchy

Abstract: *The language of medieval family life and marriage positioned males by property status and females by sexual experience, sexual availability, marital status, and motherhood. This vocabulary aligned land, sex, and lineage in ways that were insensitive to the age of persons, and unsuited to express the idea of a romantic conjugal unit, or the modern family. The result was a strong sense of patriarchal possession, constrained by reciprocal duties. Patrimonial land was a living gift held in stewardship, signifying permanent relationships between people.*

Ryan, Patrick Joseph. *Master-Servant Childhood: A History of the Idea of Childhood in Medieval English Culture.* Basingstoke: Palgrave Macmillan, 2013. DOI: 10.1057/9781137364791.

A distinctive European family pattern seems to have emerged during the Middle Ages defined by an aversion for the "joint-family", or co-residing, married siblings.[1] Parents might live with one of their married children in a "stem-family" arrangement, but siblings established their own households if they could. They delayed marriage during this effort, and often served within the households of others in the process.[2] The more frequently separate households were established for sons and daughters, the less frequently would elderly parents have been available for people to even consider three-generational arrangements.[3] Under such conditions, two-generational households were typical. As we shall see, this does not mean that European agrarian households of the millennium prior to 1600 fostered individualism according to modern middle-class family ideals.

There is an existing debate over regional variations in Europe, but it seems well-established that the pursuit of smaller, separate households was strong in northwestern Europe.[4] In these areas, since at least the late Middle Ages, women have married approximately ten years later than their counterparts in other agricultural societies. The possible causes and consequences of delaying marriage are debatable, but we know that late-marriage and small households emerged before the industrial revolution. They could not have stemmed from the spirit of commercial capitalism that came with the early-modern Atlantic world.[5] It seems reasonable to argue that the reverse happened: a distinctive household pattern preceded and encouraged other, later political and economic transformations.[6] Perhaps smaller households were indirectly advanced by Christianity's insistence on monogamy and exogamy (marriage outside the family). So too, the European family pattern may have been fostered by a decline in Roman slavery and the propagation of new forms of religious devotion to same-sex community in late-antiquity.[7]

The history of the vocabulary of family relations in English is consistent with the thesis that the pursuit of smaller, separate households which delayed marriage among commoners was an important, broadly shared feature of European cultures for nearly a millennium prior to the sixteenth century. Take the Old English *husbonde* and its Old Norse cognate *húsbóndi*, both referred to men as masters of households. *Husband* was formed out of words for house (*hus*), and land-owning peasant (*bunda*).[8] Its variants became more common within Middle English, as the words associated with *husband* connected householding and the possession of

DOI: 10.1057/9781137364791

land as pre-requisites for marriage – a status that many would attain late or not at all.[9]

In Middle English, *husband* became a conceptual umbrella for the complex position of "householder" as other terms in the Anglo-Saxon lexicon for men were being displaced. For example, the words *ceorl* (man, married man, lowest freeman) and *wer* (man, married man) both stood for married men in the Anglo-Saxon Gospels (995), but these words were not used to name householders.[10] In passages naming the heads of households, variations of the more august term *ealdor* were used – giving the sense of one with authority: a superior, a parent, an elder, a primogenitor. Four hundred years later, in Wycliffe's Middle English translation (1395), versions of *husband* filled all three positions.[11]

As the Middle English *husband* came to mean married man first, and householder secondarily, both senses continued to carry the connotation of working and possessing the land. We get this in the lowland Scotch term *husbandland*. It named a section of tillage (a *virgate*) farmed by tenants, as opposed to land worked by the lord's own bondsmen (*villeins* or *famuli*). *Husbandmen* were not servile, bound serfs tied directly on the domain of the Manor (*demesne*). They were tenant farmers and freeholders without nobility, similar to *yeomen* (14C, from Anglo-Saxon words for young + man) and *franklins* (12C, medieval Latin, free + ling). Yeomen and franklins were just beneath the lowest class of noble birth – later called *gentlemen*.

Husbandmen occupied a space between gentry and bondsmen, whether they were freeholders (yeoman or franklin) or tenant farmers, and they obtained power by possessing and working land with their families and servants.[12] They were able to mount their own households, pay the tithes and taxes, and secure privileges by paying fees – such as *merchet*, the duty owed to the lord for permission to marry a servile woman. In turn, securing a good marriage would advance the strength and independence of a husbandman's house through the immediate addition of his wife's labour. Her familial ties and the children she bore would also improve their household position. In its various uses by the late-medieval period, *husband* carried connotations of masculine power to claim women, to sire children, to craft tools, to erect structures, and above all, to till the land.

Husband and its offshoots were part of a land-sex-marriage word complex consistent with a pattern of families vying to create small sustainable households. Siblings preferred not to co-reside with each other as adults,

DOI: 10.1057/9781137364791

and the marriage system was relatively open, but it usually depended on making a household upon the land. It was only one of many terms (as will be shown) that established a language of patriarchy diffused among ordinary fathers, rather than one relying upon a claim to a noble lineage.

Small households relied upon family networks. Kinship provided security and material benefits that were necessary for survival. Unsurprisingly, those already vested with some property, skills, and connections were in a better position to expand their familial network. Among late-medieval English commoners, free and tenant husbandmen (87%), along with artisans/merchants (80%), achieved marriage far more often than men without their own land or shops: labourers (62%) and servants (30%). If their houses were productive, these small-holders would be able to pay *heriot*, the duty due the Lord whenever property changed hands (by death, inheritance, or sale). They could pass holdings onto to children or other kinsmen, gratified in their sense of belonging to kin who would remember and pray for them after death.

Husbandmen were less mobile, their households contained more servants and their young-adult children resided longer with them than most Englishmen.[13] It is not difficult to explain why. By definition, husbandmen held "sufficient property to support a family". Social historians have imagined these small farmers as the "backbone" of the medieval governing order overseeing the reciprocity between householding, the possession of the land, the rights of marriage and legitimate kinship.[14] This is not said to imply that the patriarchal assumptions which framed the husbandman's position fostered contented simplicity without struggle.[15] Quite the reverse, the possibility that a family could achieve the status of husbandmen set them the task of vying with others and among themselves. Nor is it said to imply that men created households alone. Women strove to create and recreate these households with men, or to secure a household without them when this was possible.[16]

Historical calculations suggest that no more than half of the husbandmen of medieval England would have held land adequate to support a family.[17] It is reasonable to imagine that most small householders struggled, improvised, compromised, and often failed in their attempts to achieve an adequate (the early-modern word is *competent*) household. If no one was "free" from the structures of feudalism, *husbandmen* possessed a modest but still visible means to negotiate its terms. Many other men, women, youths and children – especially those bound to manorial

DOI: 10.1057/9781137364791

or religious houses – lived with fewer options.[18] Medieval legal practices such as *childwite* (a fine payable to the manorial Lord for pregnancy outside of marriage), or *leyrwite* (the manorial fine for fornication) are particularly sharp examples of the aristocracy's and the church's attempts to exercise dominion over the very bodies of servile workers.[19]

Controlling family formation (love, sex, pregnancy, cohabitation) during any period of time is nearly impossible for any number of practical reasons. Yet, there is something more interesting than this. The policing tool – the ritual and institution of marriage – was built upon legal and theological assumptions that distributed power over family formation among competing authorities. One pillar of marriage stemmed from the Roman legal idea that it was only legitimate if based on *consensus* (agreement between the families) and *maritalis affectio* (intent to become married).[20] A second pillar was grounded in the Hebrew scriptures. The purpose of marriage was the procreation of children – the generation of kinship and lineage.[21] A marriage existed only in *una caro* (one flesh). As St. Paul put it in Wycliff's Middle English translation, "The womman hath not power of hir bodi, but the hosebonde; and the hosebonde hath not power of his bodi, but the womman."[22]

The deeply rooted tension between choice and devotion in marriage (down to our very bodies) rightly draws contemporary attention, but there was a third pillar of medieval and early-modern marriage that should not be ignored. Access to land and property necessary to marry is signified in the word we use in English to name a married man: *husband*. Being a legitimate *husband* and *wife* (*father* and *mother*) required means of making a household. Status upon the land was more important than age for maintaining legitimate family relations. There was little legal recognition of persons or families standing outside the law of land tenure. During the Anglo-Norman period, land tenure was not only "fundamental to the power of the aristocracy, [but] more locally to lesser men as well".[23] The Latin term *villenagium* stood for both the peasants and the land they worked.[24]

The hierarchies of land and labour that determined legitimacy in medieval England were not introduced by Norman invaders. Among Anglo-Saxons, land was granted to establish an ongoing debt of service of the vassal to his lord; land carried a unique "power of subordination".[25] Take the Anglo-Saxon *hægsteald, hehstald, hagusteald,* a term for youths in distinction to *ealdor*. It was drawn from Germanic words for a fenced place (*haga*) and for possessor (*steald*). A number of Latin and Germanic terms similarly represented household power (*res familiaris*) with the idea of the hedge, the fence, the court or other enclosed structure that stood as a legal barrier to *res publica*.[26] The root sense of *hægsteald* referred to plots too small to establish a household, that is, to the small patches of land given to younger sons. These younger sons might be retained as warriors by their elders, or they might serve another lord who indeed could mount *res familiaris*.[27] *Hægsteald* would have difficulty marrying and creating a household, and so the term named men who were warriors, bachelors, virgins or priests.[28] It was a word for youth, but the conceptualization of age-relations as named by *hægsteald* was inseparable from practices of land use, tenure, marriage, sexual relations and master-servant householding.

Economic historians have argued persuasively that free status alone did not carry a positive connotation, unless it came with a competency of land.[29] One might summarize the larger situation in very rough terms. All of the land of England had been settled, chartered, or otherwise granted between the seventh century and the *Domesday Book* (c. 1086).[30] When holding land was the key to power and all the land was claimed, the distinction between a free and tenant holding was significant mostly as an extension of the size and quality of those holdings. We have records of peasants accepting greater servility to a Manor in order to improve their household viability. If a husbandman's long-term situation was untenable, he might marry a villein or bonded woman to obtain access to land through her familial or manorial ties. It seems likely that for most peasants, the immediate details of rents, tithing, potential yields (land quality), fixed capital (mills, buildings, etc.) were more important than whether they were – technically speaking in modern terminology – free or tenant holders.[31]

If the origins and uses of terms such as *husband* and *hægsteald* positioned males by their possession of the land, the Anglo-Saxon words for females named them relative to their possession by men – their sexual, marital, and labouring relations with men who held land or other important forms of property. When *hægsteald* was used for a female youth the emphasis was on virginity and chastity. Sexual positioning was the most obvious purpose of many terms of womanhood. The four predominant early-medieval terms for females indicated virginity, marital availability, or relationship to household heads: *dohtor* (daughter, or affectionate address to younger/subordinate female); *mægden* (youth, unmarried, servant); *fæmne* (virgin, unmarried woman); and *wif*

DOI: 10.1057/9781137364791

(woman or married woman).[32] *Fæmne*, as an indicator of non-married status, was later replaced by forms of *mægden* or *maiden* as variations of *wif* became more important.

The vocabulary of womanhood is an index for household patriarchy. A husband's control over the sexual activity of his household was "central to his authority". Court records of the late Middle Ages document domestic violence, supported in law and by the courts to enforce a master's prerogatives.[33] Yet, the same patriarchal sensibility led masters to help their female servants negotiate terms of dowry for marriage, or advance an inheritance for apprentices. These relations are encoded in the histories of Middle English words such as *yong lasce* (young lass) and *dameisele* (damsel), that located females as unmarried or as servants, and thus naming them as potential wives. *Damsel* has a Latin root in *domus* (house) and was often used to refer to an unmarried attendant from a good family. *Lasce* (etymologically unrelated to *lad*) was used to refer to younger girls or infant daughters. It may have come from the Old Norse *lasqua* or Middle Swedish *lösk kona* for an unmarried woman, with the connotation that she was unbound and/or had no permanent residence.[34]

By the late Middle Ages, *house-wife* came to designate a woman married to a man with a house – a *husband*. This is yet another example that the paternal household was the most important point of reference for the terms we are discussing. Yet, even with *house-wife* the concept of objectification doesn't help us explain the gender dynamics, because a household was not an object in the modern sense. It was a set of relations. *Wife* was a very general term which defined a woman of experience in distinction to a *maid*. A *wife* was not only a man's woman. The word helped name trades for women, such as *ale-wyffe, fishwife, oyster-wife, apple-wife*.[35] A *midwife* was also called a *childe wyf*.[36] Such terms situated women relative to what they made, traded, or the mysteries they knew – ideas distinct from, but practically involved with, familial production and sexual relations.

This thatching of gendered meanings has an obvious practical dimension; one, partially revealed by a word originally constructed to refer to a woman that spun and weaved – *spinster*. Women with access to trades such as weaving and spinning might exercise more independence from marriage; or the reverse, women without access to marriage might be required to seek such trades. For this reason the term gained a connotation for an unmarried woman by the fifteenth century, and later for an

DOI: 10.1057/9781137364791

unmarried woman past her best child-bearing years.[37] *Spinster* captures an aspect of the land-sex-marriage complex as it appears in a host of linguistically related cultures. The Middle High German term *kint* carried a relational sense of age (being younger), but when applied to females it also indicated virginity. A girl was *kint* prior to being allowed to go with strangers; at this point she became *maget* (maiden) and at marriage she was made into a *wip* (a woman). Tellingly, a never-married, but aged woman without children could still be called *kint*. A male could be *kint* only relative in age and status to his elders.[38]

It might be argued that contemporary English-speakers remain familiar with this sort of gendered linguistic play around sex and age, and that the land-sex-marriage complex is alive and well. This would be to overstate the case for continuity. At the very least, the modern sensibility has delivered a critique of these dynamics for a couple of centuries. In contrast, the pre-modern vocabulary sustained a reciprocal relationship between the bonds of friendship and the exchange of property. Among Anglo-Saxons the ceremonies of marriage were called the *gyft* of the bride by her family to the bridegroom. In return, he would provide gifts of moveable goods for her family, prior to assuming *mund* (authority) over the bride.[39] A late tenth or early eleventh-century text "concerning the betrothal of a woman", as well as two contemporaneous marriage agreements, suggests a practice (among families controlling the land) of specifying terms for a woman's endowment, and other forms of security, as part of nuptial agreements. Certain lands are hers upon the marriage. She should be entitled to half of the estate upon her husband's death, and all of it if they have children.[40]

Across the medieval period, the lord-vassal relationship of devotion and loyalty was instantiated by a variety of economic exchanges including land grants, living accommodations, moveable wealth, and services. The twelfth-century Anglo-Norman Bishop Nigel of Ely drew upon the cultural reservoir that mixed household, land, and personal devotion when he ordered his vassals to obey "just as you love me and the fee you hold of me."[41] The Howdenshire Poll Tax of 1379 named children as "servants" along with other workers of their father's household.[42] Another included entries accounting for members as "a daughter or a slave".[43] For tax purposes the relation was the same. Belonging to a household was a general principle of *both* productive and affective ties. When interdependent household networks provided a measure of security, it was inseparable from the highest ideals of friendship reciprocity.[44]

DOI: 10.1057/9781137364791

Learning to make or serve a household, rather than taking responsibility for oneself, constituted growing up under master-servant relations. Take the word *avowed*, which came into English in the thirteenth century as a noun from the Old French *avoué*, rooted in the Latin term for *advocate*. An *avowed* was a protector, a master, a patron – someone who was bound to *espouse* or speak with authority on your behalf. Only in the middle of the seventeenth century did the word take on its modern sense of the action of claiming one's own ideas or actions (or later still "voice") – what we call *self-acknowledgment*.[45] There was relatively little space or apparatus in the structure of medieval life to belong to one's self, to espouse the individualized self, or to foster, attend to and care for a selfhood detached from master-servant relations. As Frederic W. Maitland put it succinctly more than a century ago: feudalism is the "denial of [the public/private] distinction".[46]

The weakness of the modern legal distinction between public and private was written into the structures of peasant houses. From the early fourteenth century, two categories of peasant structures might be identified: the longhouse and the courtyard farm. The courtyard farm contained multiple buildings associated with greater wealth and allowing for generational divisions to be maintained with the benefits of close proximity. The longhouse was a humble dwelling, rectangular in shape with one interior wall. The wall did not divide bedroom life from living space to separate sociability from sexual intercourse.[47] On one side of the structure was the *býre* for livestock, the other included a hearth for the people. The two kept each other warm and alive.[48] Peasants put a great deal of energy into producing grain and raising livestock, and relatively little into securing what moderns might call the accoutrements of "privacy". When compared to later centuries, they held less furniture and fewer personal affects.[49] It seems reasonable to suggest that their sense of themselves was aligned with the open layout of the longhouse with its separate space for keeping animals without a private space for the marital bed. This does not endorse Lawrence Stone's impression that pre-modern England was a "low affect societ", but it supports a point that can be distilled from his work: a modern dualism between labour and love, or a psychological distinction between self and other, were not the governing dimensions of the cultural landscape.[50]

The history of the word *family* supports this conclusion. Our use of the term *family* for a conjugal unit has no direct Anglo-Saxon or Middle English equivalent. The same was true for the Normans, and other French dialects.[51]

DOI: 10.1057/9781137364791

The term entered English directly from the Latin *famulus* – meaning servant. Previous to indicating blood and marital ties (beginning in sixteenth
century), the word referred to the Manorial lord's bondsmen.[52] The phrase
"kith and ken" drew on the concept of familiar persons (friends and family)
as early as the twelfth century, where it was used to name worldly relations
that were supposed to be less important than spiritual life.

The closest Anglo-Saxon terms for the Latin *familia* are various words
surrounding the idea of house and land. *Hiwan* and *hiwen* mixed the
idea of property or labour relations with a sense of colouring or making, and marriage. *Hid* was land, but not a measured, alienable quantity
of it, so much as a holding necessary to constitute a house. The term
hire indicated household relations of labour, as in Ine's seventh-century
law code where the husband *hired* wife, children, servants, or others.[53]
These were words of devotion and service more than kinship. Variations
of these terms applied to large monastic houses which were (of course)
not kin groups, to royal houses which were hardly nuclear, to Jesus'
bond with his apostles which was defined in opposition to blood-ties,
and figuratively to Satan's demonic court which stood in opposition to
God's dominion. In sum, these terms referred to binding unions that
were affective and spiritual, as well as political and economic. There
was no modern family ideology supposing an alienation of the former
pair of ideas from the latter, and therefore usage did not differentiate
along this pathway.[54]

Interestingly enough, the etymological components of the Middle
English *matrimony* (matri + mony) come from the Old French term
for property inherited from one's mother. The term may be a remnant
of bilateral (paternal and maternal) inheritance practices which pro-
gressively faded after about 1000 AD across Europe.[55] A documented
decline in will-making by English women from 1250 to 1550 would
be consistent with a notable hostility of common law toward women's
legal personhood during these centuries. It seems likely that the
declining legal status of women metastasized into the doctrine of
coverture – the idea that her property rights did not extend beyond
the "ornaments of her head", but were covered by father, husband, or
some other paternal figure.[56]

Contrary to the etymological components of the term *matrimony*, by
the late Middle Ages in England, children conceived in marriage inherited
property almost exclusively through their paternal line. An exclusively
paternal understanding of lineage emerged with a legal designation, *filius*

DOI: 10.1057/9781137364791

nullius ("the son of nobody"), for a child born of a woman without a husband.[57] Patrilineality was intensified by the Norman practice of *primogenitor* (a medieval Latin term for first born child) which constrained estate inheritance to eldest sons. So too, *entail* or *fee-tail* (Middle English *entaile*, *entayle, feudum talliatum* – derived from the French "to cut") originated in the late thirteenth century requiring landed estates be granted to a lord's children upon his death. Lands could not be sold-off by a lord.[58] If the lord died without an heir, it returned to the crown or another initial grantor.

A number of family practices reveal that affective and productive relationships were assumed to be one and the same. The common practice of *dowry* (entering the language in the early fifteenth century) or a substantial gift from the bride's family to the groom's estate, and agreements between families that provided for a widow's annuity upon her husband's death (*jointure*), continued the very old arrangement of marriage as a means of maintaining viable productive households.[59] The practices of inheritance, in Lawrence Stone's estimation, made the marriage (particularly of the eldest boy) "the most important strategic decision of a generation" by the late Middle Ages. Match-making and inheritance rules reinforced class endogamy, patriarchal control, and (in Stone's view) decentered individual affections from the formation of families and households.[60] No doubt, sexual pleasure or companionate friendship flourished between many husbands and wives, but these properties of personal sentiment were not the organizing structures of "open-lineage" families. The very terms *marriage* (the status of things bound together), or *wedlock* and *wedding* (the action of pledging or binding together), or *spouse* ("to claim" from the French *espouse*) indicate that the primary goal of the medieval and early-modern life-course was to bind together persons and property from two households under paternal authority to make a third.[61]

With the Fourth Lateran Council (1215), the Church proclaimed marriage to be a sacrament as nearly 10,000 parishes established a territorial presence across England.[62] Clergy should preside, partners above seven years of age should consent, and prohibitions against polygamy and consanguinity should be upheld. The wedding ceremony was to begin at the church doors; met by an unmarried, celibate priest, the sanctification of the union would only proceed if they were allowed into the house of God.[63]

The intrusion of the Church into marriage carried important consequences. It narrowed the definition of an heir for the royals at a time when neither geographic proximity nor cultural ties were as important

DOI: 10.1057/9781137364791

as marriages for securing "the primary source of territory, sovereignty, and alliance, and the major business of medieval diplomacy."[64] For commoners, the implications of sacramental marriage are less clear. Perhaps over time, it reduced the power of property restrictions by giving greater legitimacy to the consent of marital partners.[65]

The sacramentalization of marriage also posed a dilemma. Was the foundation of families and the authority that came with them to be vested in the will of the bride and bridegroom, or was marriage as a whole subject to a competing group of *fathers*: ordinary fathers and husbands, the parish clergy, the Manorial Lords, the Church (the Bishops), or the King? It seems to me that the later position was the strongest until the nineteenth century. Without dismissing the primacy that Christian doctrine gave to consent, we might recall the blunt force of the Middle English proverb: "A mayde (maid or young woman) schuld be seen, but not herd."[66] Consider too the more subtle fact that the word *bride* (Anglo-Saxon *bryd*) shares a wide set of Germanic cognates that all meant "daughter-in-law". Certainly, the church supported the requirement of the bride's consent, but her subject position had been named from the perspective of her husband's family and her economic position was wedded to a network of kinship and service. The corresponding term *bridegroom* has a more difficult etymology. In English the concept begins with the Anglo-Saxon word, *brydguma* (*guma* = man), which is a common compound with many Germanic cognates naming a soon to be married male as the "bride's man". In early Middle English, it became *brydgome* or *bridgome*, but in the late Middle Ages a different word *grome* (the servant boy who cares for the livestock) replaced the obsolete *gome*. It is unlikely that this was merely a spurious corruption as so many words denoting "young male" or "young female" have a complex morphology relating them to the concept of "servant".[67] In any event, the history of *bride* and *bridegroom* are marked by the power dynamics of kinship and master-servant relations of labour within households.

Certainly marital and sexual consent between men and women was necessary to strengthen and legitimate family ties, but the institution of marriage was not structured around the idea of consenting adulthood during the Middle Ages. Sex and marriage was structured around the possession and use of land and other forms of productive property. This is to say something more than property structured choice, but master-servant patriarchy certainly did structure marital decisions. A widow's

DOI: 10.1057/9781137364791

economic fortunes influenced the likelihood that she would remarry in a direction precisely the opposite of property-owning men. The better her economic position, the less likely she would remarry.[68] Likewise, fertility may have risen in late-medieval England when land was more widely available to men, but economic options for women to earn wages outside of marriage became more constrained.[69]

The inseparability of the ideal of consent from master-servant property relations in the politics of sex and marriage appeared in an early fifteenth-century legal dispute from York, as reported by Jeremy Goldberg. A new husband named John Waryngton claimed he had been coerced into marrying Margaret Barker by their former mutual master John Bown. In return, Waryngton was accused of seducing a number of female servants. If so, this was probably in direct violation of his apprenticeship agreement, and certainly it contravened Bown's sense of authority as master of the house.[70] Bown claimed that Waryngton had promised Barker marriage, after which the couple had engaged in sexual relations under Bown's roof. Their illicit relations were an insult to Bown that only a marriage could set right. Bown admitted that he had demanded that Waryngton make good on his promise. Inadvertently, this helped Waryngton gain an annulment of the marriage contract, as the court ruled that Waryngton had been married against his own will.

The case offers a limit-test for the master's coercive power, but it also suggests something about the persuasive power of the idea that holding a house should serve as a pre-requisite for legitimate marriage. At trial, Waryngton denied that he seduced other servants, or attempted to breach a promise of marriage. He claimed that he had only courted Barker by saying he would like to marry her if Bown was "sufficiently good and generous to him", so that he might establish himself. This appears to have been a sort of bargaining position, a condition necessary to make them respectable in the triangle of relationships between Bown (the surrogate father), Waryngton his apprentice, and Barker his maid servant. Waryngton emphasized this relational element by saying that not even his own father could persuade him to freely marry without the means to establish his family. In Goldberg's estimation, it was likely that Waryngton could "hardly conceive of marrying without having already obtained access to a workshop", and the court probably shared this assumption. This was a bad match, contracted without a consensus among the parties. Waryngton won his case.[71]

DOI: 10.1057/9781137364791

Land and moveable property were the material foundation for line-age, legitimate sex, and marriage. The point might be expanded by the parallel claims that the sense of the self was rooted in property relations, and that consent was difficult to separate from the concept of consen-sus. We should not assume, however, that a family life openly rooted in the possession of land and moveable property fostered unemotional spaces of existence. The testimony of the early nineteenth century parracide, Pierre Rivière, makes this point brutally clear.[72] These are complex interpretive issues, but there is no doubt that medieval mar-riage was the key ritual for building consensus, exchanging property, forming households, and establishing recognition of kinship. Focusing on France, Georges Duby made a point in terms that might be applied widely to medieval Europe: "Fertile marriage was the bedrock of social order. There was no house without marriage, no marriage without a house."[73] Its centrality was enhanced when it became a sacrament of the Church in the thirteenth century. The sanctification of marriage complicated and intensified a question that would become essential to early-modern theological politics: what were and who was entitled to the rights of a legitimate *father*?

The term came into English from Anglo-Saxon with widespread Germanic cognates (*fæder, feder, fader, veder, vader*, etc.). It carried mul-tivalent connotations; a *father* was male parent, protector, creator, author, ancestral patriarch, and God.[74] With increasing Church regulation of ordinary families between 1200 and 1600, the Middle English word came to be applied to early Christian writers (the *Church Fathers*), and then to the Bishop of Rome (*the holy father*), who had been called *papa* (later the Pope) in post-classical Latin. In time, other bishops took the title of *father* (*right reverend father*), and eventually this was extended to ordained priests as a group. The appellation could be used for town fathers, guild fathers, all the way up to the King himself. By the early sixteenth century, *fathers* in various guises controlled the taxes, tithes, apprenticeships, ceremonies, permissions, dowries, land, and monies which determined access to marriage, household viability, and family formation and continuity.

The study of historical semantics is not a search for causes, but an investigation of changing discursive structures. The vocabularies of Anglo-Saxon, Middle and early-modern English family life as a whole are an index of patriarchal possession. They were part of a larger lan-guage of paternalistic authority binding heaven and earth. We might

DOI: 10.1057/9781137364791

misconstrue this if we read possession as nothing more than the legal right of a free subject to choose to alienate property at a market price. Ownership was a relationship between persons, not merely a relationship between persons and things. The introduction of *bocland* (property which could be sold) during the eighth century as an alternative to the ancient Anglo-Saxon *folcland* (a form of inalienable kinship property) did not mean that a market in land sales was being created, or even desired. It may have preserved the purposes of *folcland* itself – the independence of households threatened by domination of kings.[75] So too, the great lords of the aristocratic and church houses of the High Middle Ages held lands as custodians of a trust subject to the obligations within tenancy, primogenitor, entail, and jointure.[76]

Patrimony conferred stewardship.[77] Across a thousand years of English history, those who controlled the land were not connected to it in the diminished sense of commodity exchange. Land grants were "total transactions" with religious and moral dimensions that were inseparable from the legal and economic ones.[78] The terms for removing tenants, preventing sons from inheriting tenancy or ending the lord-vassal relationship (*escheat, distraint, forfeiture, warranty*) were limited, temporary, and/or difficult to exercise. In John Hudson's estimation, a tenant was secure in his holding provided he demonstrated loyalty, and those "lower down the scale enjoyed greater security, in many instances even surviving the fall of their lords."[79] Anglo-Norman aristocrats allowed land to be exchanged so long as the transaction was duly recorded under the authority of their courts. The land was "surrendered" to the lord by one holder and "granted" by the lord to the next.[80]

As it was for the ancients, the land of medieval England was a living gift held in tenure, under various forms of God's regency or ancestral worship.[81] This animated understanding of land held in tenure became weaker and weaker in the late-medieval period as rents replaced feudal services by 1500. The commodification of land made way for enclosures for wool production, the seizure of the monastic houses in the 1530s and 1540s, and finally by the Act to Abolish Land Tenure in 1660. If a transformation of the meaning of ownership and property paved the way for a crisis in the overarching aristocratic and clerical patriarchy, it nevertheless strengthened the positions of ordinary fathers which was inherent for many centuries in the land-sex-marriage word complex. By the late eighteenth century, Blackstone could call the diffusion of patriarchy onto the landscape of everyday life "the empire of the father".[82]

DOI: 10.1057/9781137364791

Notes

1   See Peter Laslett (ed.), *Household and Family in Past Time: Comparative Studies in the Size and Structure of the Domestic Group Over the Last Three Centuries in England, France, Serbia, Japan and Colonial North America, with Further Materials from Western Europe* (Cambridge, UK: Cambridge University Press, 1972); Jack Goody, Joan Thirsh, and Edward P. Thompson (eds), *Family and Inheritance in Rural Western Europe, 1200–1700* (Cambridge, UK: Cambridge University Press, 1976); Catherine B. Silver (ed.), *Frederic Le Play on Family, Work, and Social Change* (Chicago, IL: University of Chicago Press, 1982); Antoinette Fauve-Chamoux and Emikio Ochiai (eds), *The Stem Family in Eurasian Perspective* (Bern: Peter Lang, 2009); Steven Ruggles, "Stem Families and Joint Families in Comparative Historical Perspective," *Population and Development Review* vol. 36, no. 3 (September 2010): 563–577.

2   The issue was identified in the seminal essay by John Hajnal – "European Marriage Patterns in Perspective," in D.V. Glass and D.E.C. Eversley (eds), *Population in History: Essays in Historical Demography* (London, 1965): 101–143. Mary S. Hartman explained the issue well in *The Household and the Making of History: A Subversive View of the Western Past* (Cambridge, UK: Cambridge University Press, 2004): 1–33.

3   See Steven Ruggles' analysis of "preference" and "incidence", in "The Transformation of American Family Structure," *American Historical Review* vol. 99, no. 1 (February, 1994): 103–128.

4   P.J.P. Goldberg, *Medieval England: A Social History, 1250–1550* (London: Hodder Arnold, 2004): 13–28; and, "Family Relationships," in *A Cultural History of Childhood and Family in the Middle Ages* edited by Louise J. Wilkinson (New York: Berg, 2010): 23–24.

5   Tamara Hareven, "The History of the Family and the Complexity of Social Change," *American Historical Review* vol. 96, no. 1 (February 1991): 95–124.

6   A point made forcefully by Hartman in *The Household and the Making of History*. Also see, Alan Macfarlane, *Marriage and Love in England: Modes of Reproduction 1300–1840* (New York, NY: Oxford University Press, 1986).

7   David Herlihy, *Medieval Households* (Cambridge, MA: Harvard University Press, 1985): 56–78; Pierre Bonassie, *From Slavery to Feudalism in South-Western Europe*, trans. Jean Birrell (New York, NY: Cambridge University Press, 1991); Jean-Pierre Devroey, "Men and Women in Early Medieval Serfdom: The Ninth-century North Frankish Evidence," *Past and Present* vol. 166 (2000): 3–30.

8   Unless otherwise noted the etymological analysis and semantic generalizations offered in this study are based upon the following historical dictionaries: the OED – *The Oxford English Dictionary. The OED Online* (Oxford University Press, 2012) http://www.dictionary.oed.com; the

DOI: 10.1057/9781137364791

MED – *Middle English Dictionary* edited by Frances McSparran and Paul
Schaffner (Ann Arbor, MI: University of Michigan, 1998) available online
http://quod.lib.umich.edu.proxy1.lib.uwo.ca:2048/m/mec/; the DOE –
Dictionary of Old English: A to G online, edited by Angus Cameron, Ashley
Crandell Amos, and Antonette di Paolo Healey *et al.* (Toronto: Dictionary
of Old English Project 2007) http://tapor.library.utoronto.ca/doe/dict/
index.html; and Joseph Bosworth, *An Anglo-Saxon Dictionary, Based on the
Manuscript Collections* edited and enlarged by T. North Cote Toller (Oxford:
Clarendon Press, 2009).

9   See Eric Stanley, "The *familia* in Anglo-Saxon Society: 'Household,' rather
than 'Family, Home Life,' as Now Understood," *Anglia* vol. 126 no. 1 (2008):
37–64.

10 Unless otherwise indicated, I have used the compilation of Anglo-Saxon
gospels as they appear in R.M. Liuzza ed., *The Old English Version of the
Gospels: Volume One – Text and Introduction* (Oxford: Oxford University Press,
1994); and Joseph Bosworth (ed.), *The Gothic and Anglo-Saxon Gospels in
Parallel Columns with The Versions of Wycliffe and Tyndale* (London: Reeves &
Turner, 1888).

11 Joseph is Mary's *wer* and the woman who speaks with Jesus at the well
has had many *ceorlas*. See John 5:15–18; and Matthew 1: 16–19. For passage
regarding householding see Matthew 8:5; 20:11; 21:33; Luke 12:39; Mark 10:16;
13:27, 35.

12 Barbara Hanawalt stressed the distinction between free yeoman and tenant
husbandmen, while I am persuaded by P.J.P. Goldberg and Michael Postan
who treat the term more generally and place emphasis on the quality of
holdings.

13 P.J.P. Goldberg, *Medieval England: A Social History, 1250–1550* (London: Hodder
Arnold, 2004).

14 Michael M. Postan called the husbandman a "characteristic type" of peasant
in "Medieval Agrarian Society in its Prime: §7. England" in *The Agrarian Life
of the Middle Ages* (London: Cambridge University Press, 1966): 619–620.
Cambridge Histories Online. Cambridge University Press. [Accessed January
17, 2011] DOI: 10.1017/CHOL9780521045056.014. Goldberg, *Medieval England,*
92–94, 98.

15 P.J.P. Goldberg, "Family Relationships", 26–27.

16 Judith M. Bennett, "Medieval Peasant Marriage: An Examination of
Marriage License Fines in *Liber Gersumarum*," in *Pathways to Medieval
Peasants* edited by J.A. Raftis, *Papers in Medieval Studies* 2 (Toronto Pontifical
Institute of Medieval Studies, 1981): 193–246.

17 Postan, "Medieval Agrarian Society in its Prime," 612; Robert Fossier, *Peasant
Life in the Medieval West* trans. by Juliet Vale (New York: Blackwell Publishing,
1988): 146.

DOI: 10.1057/9781137364791

18   Georges Duby, "Private Power, Public Power," in *A History of Private Life: Revelations of the Medieval World – Volume II* edited by Georges Duby, trans. Arthur Goldhammer (Cambridge MA: The Belknap Press of Harvard University Press, 1988): 21–25.

19   Judith M. Bennett, "Writing Fornication: Medieval Leyrwite and Its Historians: The Prothero Lecture," *Transactions of the Royal Historical Society* 13 (2003): 131–162.

20   Mathew Kuefler, "The Marriage Revolution in Late-Antiquity: The Theodosian Code and Later Roman Marriage Law," *Journal of Family History* vol. 32, no. 4 (October 2007): 343–370.

21   Christopher N.L. Brooke, *The Medieval Idea of Marriage* (Oxford, UK: Oxford University Press, 1989): 119–172.

22   1 Cor. 7: 4. (Wycliffe); Josiah Forshall and Frederic Madden (eds), *The Holy Bible, Containing the Old and New Testaments, with the Apocryphal Books, in the Earliest Versions Made from the Latin Vulgate by John Wycliffe and his Followers* (Oxford, UK: Oxford University Press, 1850): 348.

23   John Hudson, *The Formation of the English Common Law: Law and Society in England from the Norman Conquest to the Magna Carta* (New York, NY: Addison Wesley Longman, 1996): 86.

24   The observation was made in Frederick Pollock and Frederic William Maitland, *The History of English Law before the Time of Edward I* 2nd ed. (Cambridge, UK: Cambridge University Press, 1898): 231.

25   T.M. Charles-Edwards, "The Distinction between Land and Moveable Wealth in Anglo-Saxon England," in *Medieval Settlement: Continuity and Change* edited by P.H. Sawyer (Edward Arnold Publishers, 1976): 181–184, 187.

26   Duby, "Private Power, Public Power," 3–14.

27   Hilding Back, *The Synonyms for "Child," "Boy," "Girl" in Old English: An Etymological-Semasiological Investigation* (Liechtenstein: C.W.K. Gleerup, Lund, 1934): 171–176.

28   Kenichi Tamoto, "The Old English Words Rendering Virgo, Virginitas, and Puella in the Anglo-Saxon Gospels: The Semasiological Background in Anglo-Saxon Literature," (Ph.D. diss., Sophia University, Japan, 2001).

29   Christopher Dyer, "Standards of Living in the Later Middle Ages," *Social Change in England, 1200–1520* (Cambridge, 1989); John Hatcher, "English Serfdom and Villeinage: Toward a Reassessment," *Past and Present* vol. 90 (1981): 22–26.

30   P.H. Sawyer (ed.), *Medieval Settlement: Continuity and Change* (London, UK: Edward Arnold Publishers, 1976): 1–7.

31   Postan, "Medieval Agrarian Society in its Prime," 614–617.

32   For a wider discussion see Kim M. Phillips, *Medieval Maidens: Young Women and Gender in England, 1270–1540* (New York, NY: Manchester University Press, 2003).

DOI: 10.1057/9781137364791

33 P.J.P Goldberg, "Masters and Men in Later Medieval England," in *Masculinity in Medieval Europe* edited by D.M. Hadley (New York, NY: Longman, 1999): 62–64.

34 This assessment is based on multiple sources (OED; DOE; MED). But see the discussion in Back, *Synonyms*, 173, 184–240.

35 Helena Graham, "'A Woman's Work...': Labour and Gender in the Late Medieval Countryside," in P.J.P. Goldberg (ed.) *Woman is a Worthy Wight: Women in English Society c. 1200–1500* (Gloucestershire, England: Stroud, 1992): 126–148; Danielle van den Heuvel, "The Multiple Identities of Early Modern Dutch Fishwives," *Signs* vol. 37, no. 3 (Spring 2012): 587–594.

36 OED; also see Sally E.E. Crawford, *Childhood in Anglo-Saxon England* (Stroud, Gloucestershire, UK: Sutton Publishing, 1999): 51–52.

37 Goldberg, *Medieval England,* 109. *Spinster* became a formal legal term for an unmarried woman in the seventeenth century, but had been used in that sense from the late-medieval period.

38 James Schultz, *The Knowledge of Childhood in the German Middle Ages, 1100–1350* (Philadelphia, PA: University of Pennsylvania Press, 1995): 23–25.

39 T. M. Charles-Edwards, "The Distinction between Land and Moveable Wealth in Anglo-Saxon England," 181.

40 Dorothy Whitelock (ed.), *English Historical Documents – Volume I c. 500–1042* (London, UK: Eyre & Spottiswoode, 1955): 431, 547–548; Linda Tollerton, *Wills and Will-Making in Anglo-Saxon England* (Woodbridge, UK: York Medieval Press, 2011).

41 As quoted in John Hudson, *Land, Law, and Lordship in Anglo-Norman England* (Oxford, UK: Clarendon Press, 1994): 21.

42 P.J.P. Goldberg, "What was a Servant?" in *Concepts and Patterns of Service in the Later Middle Ages* edited by Elizabeth Matthew and Anne Curry (Woodbridge, UK: Boydell Press, 2000): 4.

43 Barbara Hanawalt, *The Ties That Bound: Peasant Families in Medieval England* (New York, NY: Oxford University Press, 1986): 156.

44 Jenny Kermode, "Sentiment and Survival: Family and Friends in Late-Medieval English Towns," *Journal of Family History* vol. 24, no. 1 (January 1999): 5–18.

45 This observation is suggested in Michel Foucault, *The History of Sexuality: Volume I: An Introduction* trans. Robert Hurley (New York, NY: Vintage Books, 1990): 58.

46 Frederick Pollock and Frederic William Maitland, *The History of English Law Before the Time of Edward I* 2nd edition (Cambridge, UK: Cambridge University Press, 1898): 230.

47 Georges Duby, "The Aristocratic Households in Feudal France," in *A History of Private Life – Vol. II – Revelations of the Medieval World* edited by Georges Duby, trans. Arthur Goldhammer (Cambridge, MA: The Belknap Press of

DOI: 10.1057/9781137364791

Harvard University Press, 1988): 63; Raffaella Sarti, *Europe at Home: Family and Material Culture 1500–1800* (New Haven, CN: Yale University Press, 2002).

48   Philippe Contamine, "Peasant Hearth to Papel Palace: The Fourteenth and Fifteenth Centuries," *A History of Private Life – Vol. II – Revelations of the Medieval World* edited by Georges Duby, trans. Arthur Goldhammer (Cambridge, MA: The Belknap Press of Harvard University Press, 1988): 444–460.

49   Carlo M. Cipolla, *Before the Industrial Revolution: European Society and Economy 1000–1700* 2nd edition (New York, NY: W.W. Norton, 1980): 107–109.

50   Lawrence Stone, *The Family, Sex, and Marriage in England, 1500–1800* (New York: Harper & Row, 1977): 93–119.

51   Dominique Barthelemy, "Kinship," in *A History of Private Life – Vol. II – Revelations of the Medieval World* edited by Georges Duby, trans. Arthur Goldhammer (Cambridge, MA: The Belknap Press of Harvard University Press, 1988): 88.

52   Rodney Howard Hilton, *Class Conflict and the Crisis of Feudalism: Essays in Medieval History* (London: Continuum International Publishing Group, 1985): 33.

53   Crawford, *Childhood in Anglo-Saxon England*, 53, 64, 109.

54   Stanley, "The *familia* in Anglo-Saxon Society," 38, 42–49.

55   Louise J. Wilkinson, "Introduction," in *A Cultural History of Childhood and Family in the Middle Ages* edited by Louise J. Wilkinson (New York: Berg, 2010): 16.

56   Goldberg, *Medieval England*, 7–8.

57   Glenn Wallach, *Obedient Sons: The Discourse of Youth and Generations in America Culture, 1630–1860* (Amherst, MA: University of Massachusetts Press, 1997): 11–12.

58   The alienation of land was limited to practices of sub-infeudation or substituting one tenant for another. Hudson, *The Formation of English Common Law,* 94–105.

59   On the growing strength of dowry during the Middle Ages see, Diane Owen Hughes, "From Brideprice to Dowry in Mediterranean Europe," *Journal of Family History* vol. 3, no. 3 (September 1978): 262–296.

60   Stone, *The Family, Sex, and Marriage*, 88.

61   Susan Dwyer Amussen, *An Ordered Society: Gender and Class in Early Modern England* (New York: Basil Blackwell Ltd, 1988): 76. Helpful essays are offered in Philip L. Reynolds and John Witte, Jr. (eds), *To Have and To Hold: Marrying and Its Documentation in Western Christendom, 400–1600* (Cambridge, UK: Cambridge University Press, 2007).

62   On the significance of the parish see, Aron Gurevich, *Medieval Popular Culture: Problems of Belief and Perception* (New York, NY: Cambridge University Press, 1988): 78–79.

63   Wilkinson, "Introduction," 12; Goldberg, *Medieval England*, 52.

DOI: 10.1057/9781137364791

64 Barbara Tuchman, *A Distant Mirror: The Calamitous 14th Century* (New York, NY: Ballantine Books, 1978): 47.

65 Brooke, *The Medieval Idea of Marriage*, 126–142.

66 "Children," *The Oxford Dictionary of Proverbs*, edited by Jennifer Speake. Oxford University Press, 2009. *Oxford Reference Online*. Oxford University Press. University of Western Ontario. [Accessed 27 April 2011] http://www.oxfordreference.com.proxy1.lib.uwo.ca:2048/views/ENTRY.html?subview=Main&entry=t90.e354

67 Grzegorz A. Kleparski, "Churls, Harlots, and Sires: The Semantics of Middle English Synonyms of *Man*," *Studia Anglica Posnaniensia* vol. 39 (2003): 50.

68 Barbara Todd, "The Remarrying Widow: A Stereotype Reconsidered," in Mary Prior (ed.) *Women in English Society 1500–1800* (London, 1985): 54–92.

69 Goldberg, *Medieval England*, 75, 87.

70 Duby, "Aristocratic Households," 82.

71 Goldberg, "Masters and Men in Later Medieval England," 58–59.

72 Michel Foucault (ed.), *I, Pierre Rivière, Having Slaughtered My Mother, My Sister, and My Brother... a Case of Parricide in the 19th Century* translated by Frank Jellinek (New York, NY: Pantheon Books, 1975): 53–121.

73 Duby, "Aristocratic Households," 56.

74 Back, *Synonyms*, 132–134; 144–145; Albert Keiser, "The Influence of Christianity on the Vocabulary of Old English Poetry," *University of Illinois Studies in Language and Literature* vol. 5, no. 1 (February 1919): 32, 66.

75 Eric John, *Land Tenure in Early England: A Discussion of Some Problems* (Leicester : Leicester University Press, 1960).

76 Stone, *The Family, Sex, and Marriage*, 87.

77 Duby, "Aristocratic Households," 84.

78 Marcel Mauss, *The Gift: The Form and Reason for Exchange in Archaic Societies*, trans. W.D. Halls (New York, NY: Routledge, 1990); J.C. Holt, "Politics and Property in Early Medieval England," *Past & Present* no. 57 (Nov. 1972): 3–52; T.M. Charles-Edwards, "The Distinction between Land and Moveable Wealth in Anglo-Saxon England," 180–187; Hudson, *The Formation of the English Common Law*, 86–117.

79 Hudson, *Land, Law, and Lordship*, 59.

80 Goldberg, *Medieval England*, 91.

81 D. Brendan Nagle, *The Household as the Foundation of Aristotle's Polis* (New York, NY: Cambridge University Press, 2006): 38.

82 For further analysis see Holly Brewer, *By Birth or Consent: Children, Law, and the Anglo-American Revolution in Authority* (Chapel Hill, NC: University of North Carolina Press, 2005). William Blackstone, *Commentaries on the Laws of England. ... By William Blackstone, Esq. Vinerian Professor of Law, and Solicitor General to Her Majesty*. Vol. Volume 1. (Oxford, M.DCC.LXV, 1765–69): 441. *Eighteenth Century Collections Online*, [Accessed 9 July 2012].

DOI: 10.1057/9781137364791

2
Boys, Girls and the Practices of Servitude

Abstract: *Service was as important as any other concept in Middle English, and patriarchal households institutionalized it. As a result, master-servant relations of labour defined what it meant to be young in medieval England. This section unpacks the centrality of servitude in medieval childhood through the history of common words such as* boy *and* girl, *and by examining the practice of apprenticeship. From Middle English to early-modern English, the language shifts toward greater specificity of age and a clearer distinction between childhood and servitude.*

Ryan, Patrick Joseph. *Master-Servant Childhood: A History of the Idea of Childhood in Medieval English Culture.* Basingstoke: Palgrave Macmillan, 2013. DOI: 10.1057/9781137364791.

DOI: 10.1057/9781137364791

Service has been called the "dominant ethic of the middle ages", and the "essence of" medieval society. As a Latinate word (*servitium*), it came into Middle English from French, it was one of the most common words used in the surviving late-medieval correspondence. *Service* referred to all kinds of work, paid or unpaid. Anything performed for one's superiors could be called a *service*, and this signified respect and loyalty. It was also a word for an appointment, a position, or what moderns would call *employment*. It could be a religious ceremony, but more specifically, the ecclesiastical text or words that were prescribed to be pronounced during the ceremony. In law or medicine, *service* was both advice and care. Above all, *service* was the term that described manorial or tenurial obligations of those who worked the land.[1]

Words linking the practices of servitude and childhood appeared commonly across many European languages during the Middle Ages.[2] For example, *lad* emerged without a connotation of age, and may have been drawn from the verb, to lead; a *lad* followed his master.[3] *Boy* came into late-medieval English and referred to any male servant, or man of low birth. The first known textual usage of *boy* is found in the mid-thirteenth century, and though its etymological origins are not known conclusively, the strongest possibilities are that it comes from: (1) the Anglo-Norman word *boie* as part of a shortening of the adjective "fettered" or the noun for "person chained"; (2) remaking the Old French *baiasse* (female servant) into a masculine form – *boiasse*; (3) directly from the middle-Dutch term *boye* for a servant; (4) or, it may have developed as a "baby word", due to the fact that the sounds of *p* and *b* are used in so many languages for "little brother", and similar concepts.[4] Whatever combination of these is correct, *boy* was a term of familial and household hierarchy for Middle English-speakers, and did not begin to carry an exclusive connotation of age until the early-modern period.

The most common early-medieval synonyms for *boy* and *lad* were Anglo-Saxon words referring to male servants or men of low rank: *cniht, cnapa, cnafa,* and *ceorl*. Before 1000 A.D., *cniht* (boy, young man, servant) was more common, but it was later displaced by *cnapa* (boy, servant). *Cniht* was etymologically connected to words referring to generation and penis, and may have been related to words for making things, such as pegs or pieces of wood, or from the sense of something thick or a clump. It is telling that *cniht-leas* meant "without servant", rather than without a male offspring. *Cniht-child* was a necessary compound word because it could not be assumed that *cniht* referred to a male child. Other

DOI: 10.1057/9781137364791

compound usages of *cniht* were formed to specify types of service: *heorþ-cniht* (servant of the hearth or domestic servant); *hiredcniht* (hired man, not lowly or servile); *horscniht* (a noble sense of a mounted servant); and *incniht* (household servant). *Leorning-cniht* was a very common term for a student or young scholar. In the Anglo-Saxon Gospels (995) the term appeared almost exclusively in reference to Jesus' disciples (15 of 16 passages) to translate the Latin *discipulus*.[5] Later we have *hierdecnapa* (shepherd boy), *munuccnapa* (boy serving to become a monk), and *þeowcnapa* (lowly bond servant).[6]

The way biblical translators handled the gospel story of the Roman officer who asks Jesus to heal a member of his house (Luke 7:7–9 and Matthew 8:6–8) shows the mixture of the concept of boy-youth-servant.[7] The Greek *pais* was initially used to name the member in need. In the Latin Vulgate (405) this was rendered as *puer*, and *puer* became *cniht* (Luke) and *cnapan* (Matthew) in the Anglo-Saxon Gospels (995).[8] Wycliff (1395) translated *puer* as *child*, but the King James Version (1611) followed Tyndale's Greek translation of *pais* to give us *servant*. The Greek *pais* was much like the Latin *puer*; it could be rendered with words indicating age, service, or generational relation. In the KJV as a whole, *pais* was rendered with a variety of words: *child* (7), *maid* or *maiden* (2), *manservant* or *servant* (11), *son* (2), *young man* (1). These were subtly interchangeable concepts, but all of the terms (*pais, puer, chiht, cnapan, child, boy, lad, maid*) were distinct from the debased positions expressed in early-modern English as *slave* or *bondsman*, written in Anglo-Saxon as *þeow*, in Latin as *servo*, or in Greek as *doulos*. The servile terms (*þeow, servo, doulos*) appeared respectively in Anglo-Saxon, Latin Vulgate, and Greek versions when the Centurion drew an analogy between his absolute power over members of his house and Christ's ability to heal the body. This suggests that the distinctions in levels of servitude which were apparent in Greek, Latin, and Anglo-Saxon became murky in the early-modern translations because the term *servant* became more diffuse, more distinct from age, while some older words in the English complex of boy-youth-servant (such as *cniht, cnapa*, and *bearn*) had disappeared from the language.

Some of the Middle English words surrounding the concept of boy or commoner (O.E. *ceorl* becoming M.E. *churl* and O.E. *cnafa* becoming M.E. *knave*) took on the pejorative meanings of ignorant, boorish, miserly, villainous, or dishonest in the late-medieval period.[9] *Churl* and *knave* lost the connotation of age in ordinary time, and only retained the idea that such persons were not (in essence) of the gentle kind.

DOI: 10.1057/9781137364791

Late-medieval English courtesy literature used the word *churl* to equate misbehaviour, not with youth, but with peasants, bondsmen, and rustics.[10] There was a corresponding increase in a sense of a person's age connoted by *boy* and *lad*. It is difficult to know whether the two trends were related. Many French terms for human beings entered English during the Anglo-Norman period, and it is possible that the older English words were relegated to more negative connotations by the Norman elite in a way that had a lasting effect upon English.[11]

Whatever the causes or precise timing, the overlap between the ideas of age and servitude was more extensive during the medieval period than under early-modern English. For example, Ælfric of Eynsham's (c. 955–c. 1010) translation of Genesis referred to Ishmael, Abraham's son by Hagar, as *cnapa* when he was miraculously spared dying of dehydration in the wilderness after Abraham casts Ishmael and Hagar out. The same term referred to the two *cnapum* who accompany Abraham to the land of Moriah to sacrifice Isaac.[12] In the early-modern English translations, Ishmael is called *childe*, *boy*, and *lad*, while those traveling with Abraham are named *young men* or *servants*.[13]

A similar shift toward age sensitivity might explain the translations of Psalm 86:16 which a twentieth-century translation has as: "Oh, turn to me, and have mercy on me! Give Your strength to Your servant, and save the son of Your maidservant" (Gideon's International). In the Latin Vulgate ("da imperium tuum, puero tuo", 405 AD), the modern "Your servant" was *puero tuo*. This passage was translated in an Old English Psalter (1000 A.D.) as *cnafa* ("syle mihte cnafan þinum"). The Anglo-Saxon version might be translated in modern English as "grant power to Your boy-youth-servant". In Wycliffe's translation the passage appeared as "yyue thou the empire to thi child". Wycliffe's late-medieval rendering of the Psalm with *child* gave way in the first complete English Bible by Coverdale (1535) to "geue thy strength unto thy servant". *Servant* has continued to be used in later English translations including Bishop's, Geneva, the King James Version, and all the way to Gideons International. The passage has retained its ancient connection to the meaning of service, subordination, humility, but the history of the translations imply an increasing necessity for separating age from these ideas.

Overstating the early-modern movement toward a distinction between the concepts of age and servitude would be unwise. A paternalistic familial hierarchy of labour continued to inform important phrases like "children of God", "sons of God", and "servants of God". These phrases became synonymous in early-modern English biblical lexicon, and they continue to resonate into the present. They may have survived because they helped name the most important of all imaginable relationships: the communion between God and Man. Social historians of early-modern England and America have documented the ways that master-servant relations organized household life. This continuity in sensibilities is obvious when one compares the early-modern phrase *chamber-chield* – a valet who might light candles, take away chamber-pots or render similar services – with the Anglo-Saxon *burcniht* – a word for servant boy likewise drawn from the words *bur* (inner chamber of a house) and *cniht* (boy or servant).[14] With all the energy that English Protestants would put into reforming childhood education, the *English Primer* of 1553 invested parents and masters with duties and powers which had long been understood as a type of regency for God's authority over Man.[15]

The long-term thatching between terms of childhood and servitude was not peculiar to English, and it was embedded in institutional developments shared across Europe. James Schultz has located a similar dynamic in Middle High German where "most of the words that designate children also designate servants".[16] Perhaps the link between boy-youth-servant has endured because of its institutionalization in the relations of labour. Take apprenticeship. *Apprentice* (L13C, *prentiz, prentis*) comes from the Old French verb *aprendre* to learn or apprehend. In Middle English, a *prentis* was bound to a master of a craft in order to learn its mysteries. The master-apprentice ideal brought with it a set of reciprocal duties. While these ideals were never easily achieved, the institution's legal foundations stood as a pillar of the economy from the fourteenth through the eighteenth centuries. It was not disestablished until industrial capitalism repositioned child labourers as mere employees, and counterpoised these child workers to the middle-class students who were (ironically) compelled to attend factory-like schools.[17]

For all the endurance of the boy-youth-servant complex, the decline of traditional practices of apprenticeship in the late eighteenth and early nineteenth centuries serve as a significant marker of change.[18] Beginning in the thirteenth century, medieval English families, with the means to do so, often bound their sons as apprentices, usually between ages 8–16 years of age.[19] During the late middle ages and early-modern period, binding children to service prior to age seven was rare, and sometimes forbidden by law. Cunningham observes that around age eight, recorded accidents of children shifted from those related to fire and play to those related to work; this might indicate a general change in children's participation in labour.[20] Yet, unlike modern institutional arrangements, entrance into apprenticeship was not age-graded.[21] It is telling that historians have been much more interested in age-grading apprenticeship than apprenticeship was interested in age-grading. Formal apprenticeship helped boys pursue the security and powers associated with craft knowledge and guild organization. Families made complimentary arrangements for their daughters, so they might gain productive skills and/or augment their dowries. For boys and girls alike, apprenticeship and service promised to increase their ties to other households and advance their eligibility for marriage.

Across five centuries, we have good evidence that a child's attainment of an apprenticeship was determined by the strength of his or her household wealth, status, and connections; and of course, gender. Approximately 15 per cent of London's mercer's (merchant's) apprentices' own fathers were members of the mercer's guild, and we can suspect that much higher proportions of these apprentices had less direct familial connections with merchants. Among the city's apprentices for skinners and tailors, one-third came from the households of merchants and craftsmen, nearly another one-third from freeholders, one-fifth from tenant farmers, and the rest from the gentry. At a given place or time, restrictions against apprenticing bondsmen (after the Black Death) or against taking on illiterate children were used to keep apprenticeship a privilege of the middling, propertied classes.[22]

In late-medieval London, there seems to have been two pathways for craft apprentices: those who paid substantial fees and might become guild members, masters of shops, and citizens of the city; and those who paid no fees, but would have to accept permanent journeyman status. From the perspective of the guilds and masters, the purpose of apprenticeship was to limit the number of persons who knew the secrets of a craft, and to control the production of goods and services. To further the governance of the crafts, in the early fourteenth century, the typical minimum term for apprenticeship set by guilds became seven years. In London, almost one-third of the apprentice contracts were for longer periods, with one in eight being set for 10 to 16 years. Guilds also controlled the number of apprentices that a household could lawfully accept. Being able to put to work, train and support multiple apprentices at one time was an indicator of considerable wealth and power. Among the powerful London goldsmiths, half of the guild membership would only be able to

DOI: 10.1057/9781137364791

take one apprentice in their entire lives, with another one-fifth taking on only two boys.[23]

Apprenticeship was one institution of master-servant households among many that defined generational, gender and labour relations.[24] Although most young male servants worked without wages, monied wages seem to have been graduated by skill, experience and gender. Apprenticeship was desirable for youths because guilds attempted to uphold familial responsibility among all the parties. Apprentices and other servants residing within the household were subject to a master's power, but they also benefited from greater assistance when incapacitated or while seeking suitable marriages, or when they were remembered in the master's last Will and Testament.[25] At any particular point in time, perhaps one in ten Londoners was an apprentice in the later Middle Ages. Other indentured persons outnumbered them by at least three to one, and enjoyed relatively less protection under yearly contracts. By the early-modern period, perhaps one-fifth of village commoners at any point in time resided as a servant within a household, but two-thirds of boys and three-fourths of girls had lived away from home as apprentices or servants during a significant period of their youth.[26] In historian Rosemary O'Day estimation, the relocation of youth into a new set of master-servant relationships was an "unifying aspect of [their] existence" across differences of class and gender.[27]

To an Italian visitor, who was probably the secretary of the Venetian ambassador, English household servitude for youths around 1500 had become venial, harsh and ignoble:

> they put them out, both males and females, to hard service in the houses of other people, binding them generally for another seven or nine years ... And these are called apprentices [who] perform the most menial offices ... every one, however rich he may be, sends away his children into the houses of others.[28]

His English friends said they bound their children so they would learn better manners; he spurred this and concluded that it only made youths more obedient workers. It is possible to read this assessment of early-modern apprenticeship and household service as evidence of "emotional distance", between English parents and their children. Contrarily, it might be read to indicate that English parents feared coddling and spoiling their young, because they loved them too much.[29] Neither of these readings hits the mark with this text. The Italian visitor was appalled that

DOI: 10.1057/9781137364791

the children "never returned" as young adults, and that they had to rely on their apprenticeship masters to help them start in business – to "open a house and strive ... for themselves". It seems to me that his critique was a way of turning his noble nose at the acquisitive, middling early-modern gentry and artisans of England for failing to uphold the classical distinction between civic virtue and ordinary work. The pursuit of happiness might result in impermanence, foster change and growth; it would run contrary to its own foundation of deference and obligations within the master-servant household.

The concerns of the Italian visitor do not appear to have been widespread. Household servitude was understood to foster virtue because it supported a larger master-servant hierarchy. Indentures of apprenticeship typically stipulated that the boy would abstain from sexual and matrimonial relations ("fornication he shall not commit, nor contract matrimony with any woman during the said term"); owed obedience and loyalty to the master ("as a true and faithful servant, shall demean himself"); must reside within the household and was prohibited from engaging in common vices ("he shall not absent himself from his said master's service day or night"); were entitled to the provision of clothing and food ("competent meat, drink, apparel, washing, lodging"); had a right to be taught the craft and spared menial labours ("the mysteries and arts of ..."); and at the conclusion of the term was entitled to a payment in kind of new clothing, land, tools and letters of support.[30] After the indenture was signed by the master and the apprentice's guardian (father), the guild fathers might examine the boy and require a ceremony of induction. The apprentices swore guild oaths which connected them to a great chain of paternal power. They served a master within a brotherhood under the authority of the city that had been granted independence by a King who was recognized by the Church which mediated the saints and provided access to God.[31] What was this, if not an ascending sequence of corresponding fatherhoods?

The apprenticed boy was a legal and corporeal presence within the master's house. He occupied a position within the hierarchy of husband, wife, son, daughter and servant. Like the system of marriage, youthful service or apprenticeship constituted an important form of exchange between households that (ideally) bound them together, differentiated them within a larger hierarchy, and affirmed status distinctions.[32] It also enhanced security and was "[p]ossibly the most important" structure for creating interdependency between families, and became the

DOI: 10.1057/9781137364791

model for dealing with abandoned, neglected or orphaned children.[33] If the apprentice ran away, his sponsors (usually his parents) could be held liable. Here, the concept of legal liability was written in language analogous to a breach of marital promise (betrothal). A master in late fourteenth century York was allowed by the guild to acquire apprentices beyond the formal maximum, "because he has no wife".[34] The resemblance between marriage, service and apprenticeship strengthened the legitimacy of all three.

Mutual obligations were not always easy for people to maintain. A majority of apprentices in late-medieval London left prior to the conclusion of their contract. Some were able and willing to buy their way out, others came to terms, many must have simply returned to family and friends in villages. City and guild records tell of masters who lacked the ability to support and train them properly, and as a result neglected, abandoned or tried to dismiss apprentices. The power of masters was far reaching because it was part of a larger pattern of master-servant childhood relations. Apprentices could be sold (though this was supposed to happen by mutual consent), or bequeathed as part of the household.[35] Their bond to the household strengthened the material and emotional support an apprentice could expect.[36] During the fourteenth and fifteenth centuries, London's masters and guild brothers were far more likely than siblings or extended kin to assume protective guardianship of a boy in the event of parental death.[37]

It has been pointed out that we have no evidence in Anglo-Saxon culture for the system of binding-out or apprenticeship that became so common in England by the late Middle Ages.[38] Perhaps childhood in early-medieval England was less differentiated by social status, and it may be that ordinary fathers had fewer powers as masters of households. This would be consistent with Publius Cornelius Tacitus' (56–117) first century *Germania*, a description of various German tribes that were ancestors of the Anglo-Saxons. Tacitus reported that they did not abandon deformed infants or otherwise sort and train young children according to the status of their birth. "The lord and slave are in no way to be distinguished by the delicacy of their brining up."[39] This is a suggestive assessment, but it should be read in terms of Tacitus' view of Rome, rather than as an ethnographic assessment of German tribal cultures.

In fact, there is little evidence to assess Anglo-Saxon childrearing. Matthew Kuefler could find only one literary reference to peasant children, and it certainly suggests a position of servitude. A school master

DOI: 10.1057/9781137364791

in the Ælfric *Colloquy*, a didactic manual written by the tenth-century Benedictine translator, teacher, homilist and hagiographer, asks a farmer if he has a mate.[40] He answers, "I have a child to goad up the oxen and he is hoarse with cold and shouting."[41] Yet, the *Colloquy* does not disregard young people; the dialogues were intended to make Latin more accessible to students. In a dialogue between a master and his pupils, the students accept the master's right to corporally punish them. But they add, "we know that you are gentle and unwilling to inflict blows on us unless we force you to."[42] When facing the question of what work is most important (religious vocations, iron work, carpentry, farming), the brightest pupil calls them to obey and accept a hierarchy of things. "So whether you be a masspriest, or monk, or churl, or soldier, perform or know this: be what you are. Because it is much humiliation and shame for a man not to want to be that which he is, and that which he should be."[43] This part of the *Colloquy* offers praise for a life outside of the Church and extends a certain respect for lay piety.

Apprenticeship and guilds were stronger during the later Middle Ages, but the underlying ideas of master-servant relations were as old as the Judeo-Christian image of the shepherd and the flock. This ancient sense of pastoral power informed the demanding regime that met young people who took on a monastic life. St. Columba, (540–615) a missionary to Ireland and an early founder of monastic rule, argued that young boys were well-suited for monastic discipline because they were quick to forgive and showed little interest in women.[44] Sporadic statistical evidence suggests that anywhere from 20–85 per cent of medieval monks were oblates bound as boys.[45] The Venerable Bede entered the monastery at age seven and reportedly spent his childhood ever in the presence of a master.

The ideal bond between *master* and *boy, servant,* or *apprentice* had a special resonance within same-sex communities, but it was also important for ordinary households. This nexus becomes readily apparent when one considers the term naming persons standing outside the master-servant household: the *vacabunda* or *vagabonds*. This word came into English in the late fourteenth century for persons unbound to a household. As a linguistic opposite of the term *husband*, *vacabunda* (idle or unoccupied or without + bond or possession) denoted those who rejected faithful service to the competent householder. *Vacabunda* stood outside the law. As such, they were positioned as dangerous, often young, masterless men and women. This was how propertied men wrote about them in England

DOI: 10.1057/9781137364791

after the dramatic ecological, demographic and political upheavals of the fourteenth century.[46]

A series of statutes from 1351 to 1430 responded to depopulation and the shortage of labour by attempting to restrict wage rates, to enforce longer periods of contracted service, and prohibit the movement of villeins away from their lords.[47] Youths working in the fields at the age of 12 were first prohibited from apprenticeship to artisans. When rural families avoided this by apprenticing boys younger than 12, authorities prohibited apprenticing boys in any town or city by families with land holdings worth less than 20s. Children and youth were commanded to stay put and do the same work as their parents had done. There was a general attempt to use statutes and ordinances (fines, public humiliation and imprisonment) to prevent mobility and market activity. The 1388 *Statute of Cambridge* restricted the movement of all beggars who were too feeble to work, allowing them to return to their home village only if their current locale would not aid them. The second-half of the fourteenth century brought expansions in sumptuary laws, prohibitions to gaming and attacks of various forms of association – all designed to support the existing master-servant hierarchy.[48] One injunction against London's journeymen tailors handed down in 1415 prohibited them from establishing a guild and claimed that these "yeoman" (freemen) lived communally as "a race at once youthful and unstable". They were said to be "unruly and insolent men without head or governance", and a threat to the entire order of things.[49]

If some young men resisted the fact that they would not be able to use apprenticeship to become householders and shopkeepers, the system was positively designed to prevent females from achieving these things.[50] Across the fourteenth to eighteenth centuries women were denied guild access. Gender exclusions seem to have intensified in the early-modern period.[51] Females could learn the mysteries of a trade legitimately if they were working alongside their husbands or fathers. If a young woman learned a trade from her father, she might find that the local guild prohibited her from teaching it to her husband.[52] If a married woman taught an apprentice, the apprentice would have to be legally bound to her husband. We know that female apprentices in medieval London learned dressmaking, brewing, silk thread making, and other trades that women were allowed to practice. Yet, Barbara Hanawalt could not find a single female enrolled as an apprentice in London's city records.[53]

DOI: 10.1057/9781137364791

It is telling that the word *girl*, though of unknown origins, was applied in Middle English to both sexes of children, young animals, or any creature viewed as having little value. Thus, *girl* was a more diffused term of subordination and low status than *boy* (male servant).[54] It has been argued unpersuasively that *girl* is related to the Anglo-Saxon word for dress – *gyrela* – or an early-modern German word – *gor* – for a small child. We know that in the fifteenth century *girl* became sex-specific, and in the next two-centuries displaced *maid* as the most important general term for the idea of "young female".[55] This semantic history is telling. In Anglo-Saxon and Middle English, variations of *maid* served to indicate a female's preparation for entrance into eligibility for marriage by denoting her virginity and position of service. The counterpart in medieval Latin was *ancilla* ("seruaunt womman") carrying the mixed connotations of youth and virginity with obligations to serve and rights to paternal protection.[56] *Ancilla* and *maid* carried assumptions about a female's life-course that the word *girl* would dilute, and perhaps help contravene. *Girl* never gave a correspondingly strong connotation of sexual status or labour service, because it became a term of age and gender. If a medieval *ancilla* and *maid* were not wife or mother, the early-modern *girl* was not old or a male. All three terms might position a female in service for late-medieval, early-modern English speakers, but *girl* could do other things. It was an important term for friendship between early-modern young women, and marked a movement away from the dynamics of the Anglo-Saxon and Middle English land-sex-marriage complex.[57]

The history of the word *wench* reveals a similar departure from a lexicon that conflated (from a modern stand-point) ideas about age, gender, sex and service. The Anglo-Saxon *wencel* was a word for a child of either sex and for a lowly servant or slave. It became a term for a female child from the late thirteenth century in certain Middle English dialects, and in later medieval centuries the word took on a pejorative sense by naming unchaste women. In the early-modern period (L16C) *wench* departed from the vocabulary of age, coming to name women of low birth or low service. Of course, most words carry more than one meaning. Speakers handle such complexity with little trouble so long as there is slight antagonism between the competing connotations within a larger governing structure.[58] The histories of *wench*, *maid* and *girl* suggest a growing need among early-modern English speakers and writers to distinguish between ideas of servitude, chastity and age. These ideas overlapped comfortably under master-servant childhood, but were

DOI: 10.1057/9781137364791

gradually relegated to different planes of human existence by modern discourses of the self.

A semantic shift does not have to be dated precisely for us to conclude that sometime between the fifteenth and the eighteenth century, *boy* and *girl* were paired as gendered terms of growing-up. This usage departed from the assumptions of the medieval boy-youth-servant complex and it signalled a more general disruption of master-servant childhood. Be this as it may, well into the early-modern period, the terms remained part of a larger lexicon of patriarchy which defined childhood in terms of labour hierarchies. The profound gender differences in the life-cycle implications of master-servant childhood should not preclude an understanding of an important continuity between medieval and early-modern times. Girls (like boys) learned to labour within a master-servant framework. From an early age most girls probably learned to spin from female kin, and to do other chores with brothers (collect nuts, carry water and firewood, etc). Formal apprenticeship may have been relatively rare for girls, but various forms of domestic servitude bound them to other households to advance their skills at carding, weaving, brewing, baking, milking, making cheese and butter, caring for poultry, as well as managing a household and keeping accounts. From the medieval into the early-modern period, unmarried young noble women found places as ladies-in-waiting serving women higher still in the aristocratic order. Through service they would learn how to present and properly order their husband's households.[59]

Notes

1   Anne Curry and Elizabeth Matthews, "Introduction," in *Concepts and Patterns of Service in the Later Middle Ages* (Woodbridge, UK: Boydell Press, 2000): xi–xxiii.

2   This is a well-documented observation. Hilding Back, *The Synonyms for 'Child,' 'Boy,' 'Girl' in Old English: An Etymological-Semasiological Investigation* (Liechtenstein: C.W.K. Gleerup, Lund, 1934): 121; Philippe Ariès, *Centuries of Childhood: A Social History of Family Life* translated by Robert Baldick (New York: Vintage Books, 1962): 366–567; John Boswell, *The Kindness of Strangers: The Abandonment of Children in Western Europe from Late Antiquity to the Renaissance* (New York: Pantheon Books, 1988): 5; Colin Heywood, *A History of Childhood* (Cambridge, UK: Polity Press, 2001): 17; Nicholas Orme, *Medieval Children* (New Haven: Yale University Press, 2001): 307;

DOI: 10.1057/9781137364791

P.J.P. Goldberg, "Family Relationships," *A Cultural History of Childhood and Family in the Middle Ages* edited by Louise J. Wilkinson (New York: Berg, 2010): 35–36.

3   Anatoly Liberman, *An Analytic Dictionary of English Etymology: An Introduction* (Minneapolis, MN: University of Minnesota Press, 2008): 135–144.

4   See Anatoly Liberman, "The Etymology of English *boy, beacon,* and *buoy,*" *American Journal of Germanic Linguistics & Literatures* vol. 12, no. 2 (2000): 201–234; Liberman, *An Analytic Dictionary,* 13–20.

5   R.M. Liuzza (ed.), *The Old English Version of the Gospels: Volume One – Text and Introduction* (Oxford: Oxford University Press, 1994) and Joseph Bosworth (ed.), *The Gothic and Anglo-Saxon Gospels in Parallel Columns with The Versions of Wycliffe and Tyndale* (London: Reeves & Turner, 1888). Matt. 10:24; 26:40; Luke 6:40; 8:9; 14:26–27; 17:22; 18:15–22; 24:33; John 6:24; 7: 11, 18; 18:15–16; 19:26–27; 20:3–4; 21:20, 23, 24. Further discussion of names for the Apostles in Anglo-Saxon poetry can be found in Albert Keiser, "The Influence of Christianity on the Vocabulary of Old English Poetry," *University of Illinois Studies in Language and Literature* vol. 5, no. 1 (February 1919): 25–27.

6   Back, *Synonyms,* 132–134; 144–145.

7   For a discussion of Anglo-Saxon gospel translations see, Liuzza, *The Old English Version of the Gospels,* xiii–lxxviii.

8   Bosworth says that Augustine of Canterbury came to England in the sixth century with the *Vetus Italica* (an earlier) Bible rather than St. Jerome's Latin Vulgate. He suggested that the Anglo-Saxon translations are based upon the former, and this was also the position of Hiram Corson, *Hand-Book of Anglo-Saxon and Early English* (New York, NY: Henry Holt Company, 1873): 505–509. Yet, others conclude that the Vulgate was the authoritative bible in early-medieval England, and it was produced and presented by Abbot Ceolfrid to Pope Gregory II in 716, prior to any Anglo-Saxon translations. See Frederick F. Bruce, *History of the Bible in English* (Cambridge, UK: Lutterworth Press, 1961).

9   See the MED, and E.J. Dobson, "The Etymology and Meaning of *Boy*" *Medium Ævum* vol. 9 (1940): 121–154.

10   Merridee L. Bailey, *Socialising the Child in Late Medieval England c. 1400–1600* (Rochester, NY: York University Press, 2012): 24.

11   Grzegorz A. Kleparski, "Churls, Harlots and Sires: The Semantics of Middle English Synonyms of *Man,*" *Studia Anglica Posnaniensia* vol. 39 (2003): 51.

12   Gen. 21: 19; 22:3; 22:19. A valuable parallel printing of a 1623 translation from Wilburgham and an Anglo-Saxon translation is offered by S.J. Crawford (ed.), *The Old English Version of the Heptateuch, Ælfric's Treatise on the Old and New Testament and His Preface to Genesis* (London: Early English Text Society by the Oxford University Press, 1969).

DOI: 10.1057/9781137364791

13 Given in order as the word choice appears in Coverdale (1535), Geneva (1560), and KJV (1611).

14 See the O.E.D. on *chamber-chield* and Back, *Synonyms*, 132 on *burcniht*.

15 Hugh Cunningham, *Children and Childhood in Western Society Since 1500*, second edition (Harlow, England: Pearson Education Ltd, 2005): 53.

16 James Schultz, *The Knowledge of Childhood in the German Middle Ages, 1100–1350* (Philadelphia, PA: University of Pennsylvania Press, 1995): 27, 40.

17 Stanley K. Schultz, *The Culture Factory: Boston Public Schools, 1789–1860* (New York: Oxford University Press, 1973); Paul Davis Chapman, *Schools as Sorters: Lewis M. Terman, Applied Psychology, and the Intelligence Testing Movement, 1890–1940* (New York: New York University Press, 1988).

18 William J. Rorabaugh, *The Craft Apprentice: From Franklin to the Machine Age in America* (New York, NY: Oxford University Press, 1986): 16–31.

19 For age estimates for apprenticeship see Angel R. Colon, *A History of Children: A Socio-Cultural Survey across Millennium* (Westport, CN: Greenwood Press, 2001): 219–220; P.J.P. Goldberg, *Medieval England: A Social History, 1250–1550* (New York, NY: Oxford University Press, 2004): 111; Hanawalt, *Growing Up in Medieval London*, 135–136.

20 Hugh Cunningham, *The Invention of Childhood* (London, UK: BBC Books, 2006): 40.

21 Barbara Hanawalt, *Growing Up in Medieval England: The Experience of Childhood in History* (New York, NY: Oxford University Press, 1993): 138.

22 Hanawalt, *Growing Up in Medieval London*, 132, 145–147; Chris Given-Wilson, "Service, Serfdom, and English Labour Legislation, 1350–1500," in *Concepts and Patterns of Service in the Later Middle Ages* edited by Anne Curry and Elizabeth Matthew (Woodbridge, UK: The Boydell Press, 2000): 21–37.

23 Hanawalt, *Growing Up in Medieval London*, 134–135, 137, 139, 144–145.

24 Stephen Henry Rigby, *English Society in the Later Middle Ages. Class, Status, and Gender* (London, UK: Palgrave Macmillan, 1995).

25 P.J.P. Goldberg, "What Was a Servant?" in *Concepts and Patterns of Service in the Later Middle Ages* edited by Elizabeth Matthew and Anne Curry (Woodbridge, UK: Boydell Press, 2000): 10–18. On the household master's powers, see Georges Duby, "Private Power, Public Power," in *A History of Private Life: Revelations of the Medieval World – Volume II* edited by Georges Duby, trans. Arthur Goldhammer (Cambridge MA: The Belknap Press of Harvard University Press, 1988): 28, 55.

26 Peter Laslett, *The World We Have Lost*, second edition (New York, NY: Scribner, 1971): 67; Cunningham, *The Invention of Childhood*, 81; Lawrence Stone, *The Family, Sex, and Marriage in England, 1500–1800* (New York: Harper & Row, 1977): 107.

27 Rosemary O'Day, *Education and Society, 1500–1800: The Social Foundation of Early Modern Britain* (New York: Longman, 1982): 4.

DOI: 10.1057/9781137364791

28   Author Unknown, *A Relation, Or Rather a True Account of the Island of England... About the Year 1500*, translated by Charlotte Augusta Sneyd (London: Camden Society, 1846): 24–25. Also see Ariès, *Centuries*, 365.

29   On the fear of coddling, see Edmund S. Morgan, *The Puritan Family; Religion and Domestic Relations in Seventeenth-Century New England* (New York, NY: Harper & Row): 77.

30   Mary Abbott, *Life Cycles in England, 1560–1720: Cradle to Grave* (New York, NY: Routledge, 1996): 175–177; Philip A. Bruce, *Economic History of Virginia*, II (New York and London, 1896): 1–2n; Colon, *A History of Children*, 220.

31   Hanawalt, *Growing Up in Medieval London*, 140–141.

32   Grant McCracken, "The Exchange of Children in Tudor England: An Anthropological Phenomenon in Historical Context," *Journal of Family History* vol. 8, no. 4 (Winter, 1983): 303–313.

33   Margaret Pelling, "Apprenticeship, Health, and Social Cohesion in Early Modern London," *History Workshop* no. 37 (Spring, 1994): 33–56.

34   Goldberg, *Medieval England*, 102.

35   Hanawalt, *Growing Up in Medieval London*, 138–140, 157–159.

36   On these elements of master-servant relations see the essays in Susan Broomhall (ed.), *Emotions in the Household, 1200–1900* (Basingstoke, UK: Palgrave Macmillan Press, 2008).

37   Hanawalt, *Growing Up in Medieval London*, Table 6, 225.

38   Dorothy Whitelock, *The Beginnings of English Society* (Harmondsworth, UK: Penguin Books, 1954): 94.

39   David Herlihy, "Medieval Children," in *Essays on Medieval Civilization: The Walter Prescott Webb Memorial Lectures* edited by Bede Karl Lackner and Kenneth Roy Philip (Austin, TX: University of Texas Press, 1978): 114.

40   For commentary and a translation of the *Colloguy* see Stephen J. Harris, "Ælfric's *Colloquy*," in *Medieval Literature for Children* edited by Daniel T. Kline (New York and London: Routledge, 2003): 112–129.

41   Mathew S. Kuefler, "A Wryed Existence: Attitudes Toward Children in Anglo-Saxon England," *Journal of Social History* vol. 24 no. 4 (Summer 1991): 830.

42   Patricia Demers, *From Instruction to Delight: An Anthology of Children's Literature to 1850*, second edition (New York, NY: Oxford University Press, 2004): 7–12.

43   Harris, "Ælfric's *Colloquy*," 124.

44   Kuefler, "A Wryed Existence," 824–825.

45   Colon, *A History of Children*, 120–125

46   A summary is provided by Given-Wilson, "Service, Serfdom, and English Labour Legislation, 1350–1500," 29–31.

47   Bertha Haven Putnam, *The Enforcement of the Statute of Labourers in the First Decades after the Black Death* (New York, NY: AMS Press, 1970), first published 1908.

DOI: 10.1057/9781137364791

48   Given-Wilson, "Service, Serfdom, and English Labour Legislation, 1350–1500," 28–29, 34–35.

49   P.J.P. Goldberg, "Migration, Youth, and Gender," in *Youth in the Middle Ages* edited by P.J.P. Goldberg and Felicity Riddy (Rochester, NY: Boydell & Brewer, 2004): 94–97.

50   For a review of this literature on this issue see Clare Crowston, "Women, Gender, and Guilds in Early Modern Europe: An Overview of Recent Research," *International Review of Social History* vol. 53 (2008): 19–44.

51   Ilana Krausman Ben-Amos, *Adolescence and Youth in Early-Modern England* (New Haven, CN: Yale University Press, 1994): 133–155; Goldberg, *Medieval England*, 102–105; Goldberg, "What is a Servant?," 68–69. The point is also emphasized by Sandra Cavallo, "Family Relationships," in *A Cultural History of Childhood and Family in the Early Modern Age* edited by Sandra Cavallo and Silvia Evangelisti (New York, NY: Berg Publishers, 2010): 15.

52   Colon, *A History of Children*, 222.

53   Hanawalt, *Growing Up in Medieval London*, 142–143; Goldberg more strongly states the inaccessibility of guild privileges to women in *Medieval England*, 113.

54   Anne Curzan, *Gender Shifts in the History of English* (Cambridge, UK: Cambridge University Press, 2003): 133–179.

55   A. Moerdijk "(Mis)use of Semantic Parallelism: Robinson's Etymology of English Girl" *North-Western European Language Evolution* vol. 24 (1994): 49–65; B. Diensberg, "The Etymology of Modern English Girl," *Neuphilologische Mitteilungen* vol. 85 (1984): 473–475; Liberman, *An Analytic Dictionary*, 94–100.

56   Goldberg, "What Was a Servant?," 1–4.

57   Jennifer Higginbotham, "Fair Maids and Golden Girls: The Vocabulary of Female Youth in Early Modern English," *Modern Philology* vol. 109, no. 2 (November 2011): 171–196.

58   Grzegorz Kleparski, "Pejorative Developments Interpreted Differently," *Kwartalnik Neofilologiczny* vol. 33, no. 1 (1986): 25–49.

59   Cunningham, *The Invention of Childhood*, 88–89. Goldberg, *Medieval England*, 93–94, 261–262.

DOI: 10.1057/9781137364791

3
Childhood Without Adulthood

Abstract: *Medieval childhood was rooted in patriarchal households and hierarchies of labour, but these structures do not constitute the whole of its semantic depth. The words most directly tied to the concept of a "child" emerged from a different matrix, conceptually split between bodily growth and lineal descent. Childhood was associated with the earth, mother and origins – with profane growth, folly and change. Yet, it was also the most powerful concept for imagining the human capacity to be adopted as servants of an eternal, perfectly fixed God. Ensconced in the mystical tension between ordinary existence and Providential design, the terms of master-servant childhood could not speak-well a discourse of individual development, socialization, authenticity or agency. It was not a means to adulthood.*

Ryan, Patrick Joseph. *Master-Servant Childhood: A History of the Idea of Childhood in Medieval English Culture.* Basingstoke: Palgrave Macmillan, 2013. DOI: 10.1057/9781137364791.

Variations of *child* (*cild, cyld, chyld, chilld, chylde, childe, schyld, chield*) appeared in English texts beginning from the ninth century, and were initially used in reference to the mother. The word came into the language with *kin* through terms for womb and pregnant woman in Old Teutonic *kilpo* and in Gothic *kilpei* and *inkilpo*.[1] Its reference point, the word *mother* (*modor, medder, modder, moeder*, etc), was derived from Germanic languages probably rooted in the baby-word or phonetic sound "ma". By the end of the Anglo-Saxon period, the multiple meanings of *mother* centred upon fertility and child care. *Mother* connoted female parenthood, sustaining care, institutional caretaker and the place of one's birth. These were concepts of belonging and obligation, but unlike the terms we have examined in previous chapters, *mother* and *child* added a sense of origins, being and becoming to the concept of service.

The distinguishing characteristic of *child* (its synonyms and variations) in Anglo-Saxon and Middle English lays in the fact that these words did not help tell a story of becoming an *adult*. Modern competent, mature, autonomous adulthood was not yet part of the prevailing discourse of being human within English. This said, the ideas of *origin* and *being* cannot be detached from concepts of *time* and *age*. From the outset, these words were disposed to transmit a concept of age (being over time) in contrast to the patriarchal household terms of labour servitude that framed both the land-sex-marriage and the boy-youth-servant word complexes. As the next three sections will show, the terms of a child-age-generation complex that arose in English prior to modernity are comprehensible only in relation to a sense of time that is unlike our own. This sensibility did not entail the idea that age was a property of individuals within a population, because it gave priority to the distinction between time eternal (or cosmic order) and the ordinary time of our perception. The associated word-complex was organized around a logic of correspondence and encouraged a search for parallels, rather than following a logic of mechanical functioning and its consequent yearning for authenticity and individual agency.

The most important Anglo-Saxon word for child was *bearn* (*bairn, barn*, etc.) – a word of Germanic and Scandinavian origins meaning "that which is born". A less common term that shared some territory with *bearn* in Anglo-Saxon was *gebyrþen* (from "to bear a burden"), but *bearn* was closer to *eafora* (from "one who comes after"). According to Hilding Back's comprehensive study, Anglo-Saxon contained comparatively few tools that could serve to designate children "in the collective" sense. One

DOI: 10.1057/9781137364791

term, *ofspring*, carried the extended sense of one's seed or semen; others were variations upon *tudor*, a word rooted in terms for being tethered to, or drawn from ancestors.[2] These terms often denoted young descendants, the phrase *wif* and *bearn* being common. They helped designate parentage and identified who belonged to a household. People belonged to households, not age-groups; and lineage was a relationship not a set of individuals.

Bearn was ubiquitous in Anglo-Saxon and it was used in phrases of pregnancy and birth such as *bearn-team* (the bearing of children) *bearn-cennice* (a mother), and *bearn-eacen* (big with child). Handling the protean-ethereal concept of lineage was the primary work of *bearn*. It could relate persons in a mystical sense of origin, as in the second birth that was signified in becoming a Christian communicant or *huselbearn* (child of the Eurcharist).[3] When Jesus called his disciples *filioli* in the Latin Vulgate, it was *uuscbearn* or *bearn* in the Anglo-Saxon Gospels (tenth century), and "Litle children" in KJV.[4] In turn, Jesus was referred to as *godbearn* (son of God), *haelubearn* (Christ child), or *sigebearn* (victorious child). On the matter of the Trinity, the Ælfric *Homilies* asked, "Hwaet is se Fæder?" (What is the Father?). He is that which "gestrynde Bearn" (begot the Son) whose essence or unity with the Father preceded his incarnation as a child born of Mary.[5]

Like *bearn*, the Anglo-Saxon *cild* was also rooted in Germanic words for womb and pregnancy, but instead of naming that which is born, the word comes from an attempt to name "that which swells". With this root meaning, *cild* primarily helped people work with concepts of growth and change over time, and only secondarily with the possession and descent (*mine cild* – my children). The *cild/bearn* distinction allowed one to more clearly speak of the materiality of one's bodily birth (existence) in contrast to the spirituality of one's lineage (essence). Jesus was the archetype, but the idea was not limited to the Incarnation. In one of its many uses, *bearn* served as the Anglo-Saxon equivalent to the later English title – "the younger". It distinguished by relative youth, any father–son pair who held the same names.[6] Here we have ideas of "descent" and "age of persons" positioning being human in time, but the mixture of the two make neither (descent or age) a property of the self.

The Anglo-Saxon *sunu* (son) was much more likely than *cild* to stand for the singular form of *filius* (child, descendent), while *bearn* predominately held the position for the plural *filii* (children, descendents).

DOI: 10.1057/9781137364791

Filius was not translated with *dohtor* (daughter), because lineage was traceable only through males. As with the land-sex-marriage and the boy-youth-servant complexes, these uses assumed masculine points of reference.[7]

In early medieval texts, *cild* often referred to foetuses, babies or very young children in the sense of their age as persons. Yet, *cild* could also stand for terms of service or lowliness, as it often did in Old English translations for the Latin *puer* (as a noun for boy or servant or child), or for *infans* (as an adjective meaning inarticulate or foolish, and standing for infancy as a noun). The sense of age was strong in these words, as it was when *cild*, *cnapa* or *cniht* were used for students and boys.

The significance of the *cild/bearn* relationship is further suggested by the fact that Anglo-Saxon poetry rarely, if ever, used the former term. *Cild* named a humble concept associated with bodily growth, unfit for speaking about the essence of things. While *bearn*, a term of descent, was common in Anglo-Saxon verse.[8] In the Anglo-Saxon Gospels, *bearn* appears in passages where the sense of lineage or a more profound generational relation needed to be invoked. For example, when the baby Jesus is pursued by Herod's men, he is a singular *cild* who escapes to Egypt, while all other children are slain (*ealle ða cild*). When Rachel, who stands for the mothers of Israel, cries out in anguish for the slaughtered infants, she weeps not for a particular *cild*, but for her *bearn* – Israel's lost generation.[9] Likewise, when John the Baptist's special relationship to Jesus is named, he is upheld as unique among *wifa bearnum* (later translations gave "children of women").[10] When Jesus teaches that his followers must leave their earthly kinship and lineage to join an eternal one, the passage tells them to abandon *faeder*, *moder*, *wif*, *bearn* (for the Latin *filios*), *broðru* and *swustra*. In the Middle English of Wycliffe, *sones* (not *bearn*) stood for the Latin *filios* in many passages including this one, because much like *bearn*, *sones* carried a sense of inheritance. Only in the sixteenth century will Tyndale set a new course for modern translations by giving the list of kinship in this passage as *father, mother, wyfe, children* (from the Greek *teknon*), *brethren* and *sisters*.[11] The Greek *teknon*, Latin *filios*, Anglo-Saxon *bearn*, Middle English *sones* were all ways to name descent and granted the right of material inheritance. *Children* may have carried a double sense of earthly lineage and growing persons for Tyndale's readers, but the distinction must have been weaker than the one made by *bearn* when it still could be deployed in contrast to *cild*. The disappearance of the *bearn/cild* distinction coincided with a general

DOI: 10.1057/9781137364791

movement in English translation of the Gospels from the Anglo-Saxon *bearn*, to the Middle English *sones*, to the early-modern *children*.[12]

The subtle interactions between the Anglo-Saxon *cild*, *bearn*, *sunu* and *cnapa* allowed for overlapping concepts of being in time (age): growth, descent, filial love, service, deference and obligation. All of these terms carried a relational sensibility, so that even during the early modern period "*child* meant more 'offspring' than an age-limited pre-teenage category".[13] Early-modern *child* was often relational, much like the contemporary use of the terms *brother* and *sister*. In modern English usage, *brother* and *sister* connote filial membership and mutual obligations. No one is a *brother* or a *sister* within themselves. Marginal phrases like the "only-child syndrome" aside, having a sibling does not resonate today as a property of the self for a young person in the way that say, being an 18-year-old does.

The modern meanings of *brother* and *sister* retain a sense of things between persons that has been weakened as the modern English lexicon of childhood as a whole has moved from relations to persons and groups. We can see an early sign of this when the Anglo-Saxon *cild* became the Middle English *child* (*chyld*, *chilld*, *chylde*, *childe*), subsumed *bearn*, and created more room for the plural Anglo-Saxon form: *children*.[14] The subtle weakening of the linguistic priority granted to the idea of lineage was not (of course), "caused" by a single word shift; we are trying to get a sense of the meaning of a gradual shift in the terms of childhood, rather than find the shift's first cause.

This task might be furthered by looking at the ability of the Anglo-Saxon *lyteling* (a term for lowly or ignorant persons rooted in "to bow down") and *cild* to stand for the Latin *parvulus* (as an adjective, meaning little, slight, young or unimportant).[15] These terms related subordination, weakness or smallness with the sense of being young. They allowed writers to effectively communicate the important Jesus saying from Matthew 18:2–5, when the disciples are told they must become (in modern terms) "like children" to enter the kingdom of heaven. In Latin this was given as "conversi fueritis et efficiamini sicut parvuli". The term *parvuli* was rendered in the Anglo-Saxon translation (995) as *lytlingas*. This term carried an association with becoming like the "humble" or the "simple", and it also fit with the remainder of a passage that threatened God's wrath upon those who mistreated the lowly and the weak. It would be as if a millstone had been hung around their necks as they were cast into the sea. A general point

DOI: 10.1057/9781137364791

comes through: one must submit to God and protect the vulnerable to win favour in heaven.

In Wycliffe (1395) being like *parvuli* would read *as litil children*. Working with the Greek (*wv ta paidion* or like children in thoughts), Tyndale (1526) would render the passage, "except ye tourne, and become as children, ye cannot enter into the kyngdom off heven".[16] The King James Version (1611) used similar words for the 51 times the Greek *paidion* appeared: *child* (25), *little child* (12), *young child* (10), *damsel* (4). Subsequent English versions have largely followed suit. The late-medieval and early-modern introduction of the word *child* into these passages maintained linkage with servitude, subordination and a lack of inherited power which we find in the Anglo-Saxon *lyteling* and the Latin *parvulus*. However, *child* has shifted meanings since the early-modern period. It no longer carries connotations of servitude well, because it brings forward associations with authenticity, development and innocent freedom from work. So, the ancient passages that drew meaning from words within an older boy/servant linkage have gained novel meanings during the past few centuries.

As was stated earlier, the case for change in the early-modern period should not be oversimplified. The early-modern translations allow us to document a departure between the terms of childhood and servitude that took place over a long time. The words most closely related to *child* continued to carry forward a master-servant sensibility into the early-modern period. Take Myles Coverdale's (1488–1569) first complete English Bible in 1535. Coverdale had no direct English word for Christianity's central metaphor for communion with God. Writing in Greek, St Paul had named the Christian's proper relationship to God the Father – υιοθεσία (*yiothesia*) – translated in the Vulgate as *adoptionem filiorum*.[17] This is the opposite of *filiorum alienorum* or heathen children (*bearn fremde* – strange children; *feondes bearn* – children of the devil). *Yiothesia* was related to the concept of "children of the church", or *ecclesiae filii* (tr. *gelaþunge bearn* in Ælfric writings) which figured Church as bride, Christ as groom, and Christians as their children. *Yiothesia* was a relationship that allowed Christians to become *filios Dei* from John 1:12 (tr. *Godes bearn* in Anglo-Saxon), appearing under various forms of "sons of God", in the Wycliffe, Tyndale, and the KJV.[18] Working with previous English and German renderings of the original Greek, Coverdale translated *yiothesia* by inventing the English word *childshippe*.[19] He has St Paul tell us that to "receave ye childshippe" is to be adopted as a son

DOI: 10.1057/9781137364791

of God. Other early-modern English translators (Geneva and KJV) rendered *yiothesia* as the "adoption of Sonnes" – an estate promised to Christ's faithful servants. These "Sonnes of God" would inherit a birth-right in the kingdom of the Father underneath the authority of Christ Himself. We can see that the terms of childhood readily indicated to the first readers of the English Bible that salvation comes to Christians as a master-servant relation of patriarchal adoption which supersedes an earthly lineage. In this passage the strongly relational words, *son* and *adoption*, seem to have preserved important master-servant elements of the medieval/ancient child-age-generation complex.[20] It is possible that *childshippe* and *adoption of Sonnes* did not maintain the conceptual space between being human in time (growth, change and existence) and the timelessness of God – at least not as well as the Anglo-Saxon *gelaþunge bearn* or *Godes bearn*.

Be this as it may, the Middle and early modern English usage of *child* or *son* was consistent with the early Christian deployment of the Latin *puer* (boy/servant) to name any baptized male regardless of age.[21] To be reborn, a Christian had to become a son or servant of God and refuse to be a slave to mammon. *Puer* was a good Latin word to indicate the linkage between purification, childhood and service to Christ. Likewise, Coverdale's Christians were told: "Yf we be childre, then are we heyres [heirs] also, namely heyres of God, and heyres annexed with Christ, yf so be that we suffer together, that we maye be also glorified together."[22] We can better comprehend the semantic continuity between what *puer* was doing in the Latin translation and what *child* was doing for the early-modern English Bible, if we recognize that the larger discourse of master-servant childhood carried the demands of a labour hierarchy much more strongly than the ages of individuals. Evidence for this has been offered throughout this essay, let me offer yet another piece. A study of twelfth-century Latin records was able to ascertain that *puer* was used to name a wide set of persons under the age of 28 years, while *iuvenis* (youth) could name anyone under 50 years of age.[23]

The phrases *children of God, sonnes of God, childshippe, Godes bearn, adoptionem filiorum*, and *υιοθεσία* spoke of something that is incommensurate with the modern concepts of individual development or age groupings. These were phrases calling forth the idea that a divine spirit was incarnate in the world because the *Father* (or creator) manifested himself through the *mother* of Christ, and remade us all into *children* of God. Taking this seriously, bringing this theological vision into the

DOI: 10.1057/9781137364791

various structures of thought and practice, required a mode of perception which might be called a logic of correspondence or a discourse of literary parallelism. By analogic reasoning, ordinary *mothers* bring *children* into their profane existence (making a fallen thing), but our essence (the human place in the *order of things*) is something claimed and salvaged by a sacred paternal lineage – a *fatherhood*. The patriarchal content of ancient Christian theology is obvious, while its logic of correspondence is often overlooked; yet, the latter is absolutely essential for grasping what separates medieval from modern childhood in European cultures.

Failure to attend to theological nuances can severely hamper our ability to read childhood adequately. For example, medievalist Nicholas Orme has pointed out that William Tyndale (1492–1536), whose English translation of the *New Testament* (1526) framed Coverdale's Bible, wrote that "a chylde... yf he crye... men styll with a poppet".[24] Orme presented this comment as evidence of a sense of care for children, but he failed to note that Tyndale was drawing a disparaging analogy between soothing a child with a doll and those who would imagine that they could so sooth the wrath of God with "ceremonies and sacrifices (the meaning and signification lost, and the cause forgotten, which God ordained them for) to flatter and please God with the gloriousness of the deed in itself".[25] Here, Tyndale was building upon a common medieval denunciation of mishandled sacramental rituals.[26] The essence of God's Will could not be circumvented by the play of material things controlled by earthly authorities. Any ceremony that inverted God's rightful master/ father position relative to Man as servant/child delivered the ultimate insult to God and disordered our position relative to Him.

What Orme presents as an example of continuity with contemporary parental sensitivity toward fussy babies, upon careful examination, reveals a sense of childhood embedded in a very different, non-mechanical discourse of the self in space and time. Tyndale was using childhood to distinguish between supplication to God's authority (prayer and sacrament) and the occult manipulation of the forces of nature (magical power). He was operating within the discursive structure of master-servant childhood and affirming the theological distinction between mere existence and cosmic essence. This drew upon medieval theological discourse, but it furthered a sixteenth-century assault against clerical intercession: the mass, confession, prayers for the dead, the consecration of structures, the churching of women after birth, infant baptism, the taking of oaths, in addition to Protestant attempts to abolish the use of a panoply of Catholic shrines, tokens and relics.

At the risk of moving beyond the scope of this study, it is worth stating that the Protestant critique of sacramental ritual as a form of magic did not entail a liberation from master-servant relations between Christians or with God. The Reformation was not a liberal revolution. Reform theologians were offended by magical beliefs and practices precisely because they believed that magic reversed the chain of being that connected Man and God. Tyndale argued that a prayer "repeated without understanding [was not] any better than a charm".[27] In Tyndale's vocabulary, childhood could be used both to signify the ideal of obedience and the inability to speak or understand truth. This discursive tension was exacerbated by a more obvious irony. The Protestant attack upon the corruption of the sacraments led them into disobedience against the Church in the name of speaking the truth. Reformers responded to this twisted web by inventing novel legal and theological arguments that would ultimately annul the traditional Christian commandment to supplicate oneself to higher powers – princely and ecclesiastical authorities.[28] It was as if they came to think that accessible translations, printing, and distribution of bibles, catechisms and other religious texts would create a word-based religiosity unencumbered with the problems of worldly power and the ambiguity of human language. Moderns cannot help smiling at a certain *naïveté* within all this, but for Tyndale, devotional artifacts could be manipulated too easily by clerics. Relics encouraged people to toy with God, and so reformers demanded these be "taken away and given to children to play with as dolls".[29]

Tyndale's critique of popular religious practices was closely associated with an ancient discourse that equated childhood with play (games and theatre), human frailty, error or unreason. We hear his child/play dualism in the Old French *anfance* (childhood) which is literally translated as "foolish talk". The idea is reflected in the old Flemish proverb, "It is no child's play or madness, it is anything but an easy task." Or we might cite the French proverb, "De fol et d'enfant garder se doit len" (one should avoid lunatics and children).[30]

Better still, Pieter Brueghel's well-known 1560 painting *Khinderspill* (*Children's Games*) displayed the ancient link between childhood and human error as a panorama of children frolicking through a village, playing scores of games. The painting serves as book-cover art for Orme's *Medieval Children* (2001), but unfortunately he treats it as an

DOI: 10.1057/9781137364791

"encyclopaedia of games", a "celebration of childhood and its ingenuity", and evidence of a universally sensitive adult-eye "devoted to [children and adolescents] entirely".[31] For Orme and others seeking an ahistorical child, *Children's Games* serves as evidence to combat Ariès' historical claims for childhood. It seems to me that reading the painting as a record of experience requires that we badly misconstrue the thematic structure of the painting. According to Sandra Hindman, Brueghel positioned childhood and the games people play in worldly time (our existence) in opposition to the essence of the universe (logos or reason) and God's will. The painting acted as a commentary on the cycle of courtship, marriage and baptism. The game of marriage, standing as the chief rite of passage from childhood to adulthood, is represented with its familiar association with the game – blindman's bluff. This signified humanity's inability to overcome outrageous fortune merely through the Church's sacramental intervention into family life.[32] Here we have a major theme of Tyndale's critique of ritual delivered within a visual medium. Given Hindman's close analysis of *Children's Games*, it would be the height of anachronism to read it in terms of the four competing modern discourses of childhood which position play as (1) a mechanism for socialization (2) scaffolding for optimizing cognitive development (3) an innocent retreat from the adult world of instrumental labour (4) a demonstration of children's competent agency as creators of their own culture.

Whenever the prevailing mode of thought follows a search for parallels (as opposed to the mechanisms of cause and effect), the mind will be disposed toward reversal, irony and paradox. And, so it was with the discourse of master-servant childhood. Children were associated with the earth, with mother and origins, and human folly; yet they also served as icons of subordination and service to God the Father. The opposition between the ideal of the Christian adopted into the perfect *childshippe* and the folly of *Children's Games* co-existed within the discourse of childhood as a generative tension. Modern thinkers have trouble recognizing the centrality of childhood for the medieval opposition between human existence (games) with Providential order (adoption), because the landscape of modern childhood is defined by an age-grouped, child-adult dualism. The next section will historicize *age* as a sense of being in time without accepting the transcendent terms of modern developmental-socialization.

DOI: 10.1057/9781137364791

Staying with the terms closely related to *childhood*, here, we can note that the ancient theme of children's folly rolled nicely into the concept of bodily vigor during youth. Youth was often situated in opposition to the wisdom of age. This notion can be found within the Hebrew *Proverbs*: "The full out joying of young men is the strength of them; and the dignity of eld men is hoariness (white hair)."[33] And we can hear it in the Italian-born knight Philip de Novara's (c. 1200–c. 1270) *Les Quatre Ages de l'homme* when he says a young man is *jovant*, "so puffed up with the natural wind of youth that fans the flames, that he is unaware of his actions and does not heed what people say about them … will overrides reason".[34] It appears in the modern French saying, "Si jeunesse savait; si viellesse pouvait" (If only youth had wisdom, and age had strength). To position youth in terms of body and age in terms of wisdom does not require a developmental theory of growth from childhood to adulthood. Its purpose was to create meaning through the contrast. The difference between correspondence and mechanics is sometimes lost in translation. This is one of the reasons why translating an ancient word, such as *adolescentia*, into modern English presents such severe difficulties.[35] *Adolescence* dramatically shifted its meaning in the early twentieth century under the emergence of a medicalizing discourse of childhood. For us, *adolescence* is a term indicating a period of individual development defined by hormonal transition, generational conflict and identity crisis.[36] As Marc Kleijwegt and James Schultz have shown, the conceptual structure of modern *adolescence* is incommensurate with ancient Latin and medieval German discourses of youth.[37]

The modern concern for establishing or clarifying the boundary between childhood and adulthood (the desire to clarify the liminal space of youth) seems out of place in the Middle Ages. In Hilding Back's forensic judgment, within Anglo-Saxon texts, "on the whole the idea 'a youth' was expressed comparatively seldom". The nearest Anglo-Saxon synonyms for adolescence are *geoguþ* or *geonga* from Old Saxon *juguþ* meaning youth in a collective sense for both sexes, and rooted in the idea of a strong body.[38] These words refer to a state of being, a time of life and movement between childhood and adulthood, but grasping the full sense is challenging. In translations of *adolescens* from Matthew and Luke in the Latin Vulgate, we find *geonga* or *geonga mann* in the West Saxon translation (995), but in the earlier Rushworth and Lindisfarne texts the word *esne* was used: meaning servile man, harvestman, day labourer rooted in the term for harvest time.[39]

DOI: 10.1057/9781137364791

Once again we find master-servant concepts woven into terms of youth that entail, but are not defined by, age relations. As John Boswell pointed out, the vast majority of people in "Western history" have lived their "lives in a juridical status more comparable to 'childhood'... [under the control of] a father, a lord, a husband, etc." The titles they are given make it "often impossible to be sure, without adequate context, whether the appellation is based on age, or status, or both".[40] Historians have spent considerable time trying to recover the "context", by cross-referencing sources so they might insert data or categories of age, and reconfigure the story into modern terms. A different response would be to admit that we, as readers, come to historical texts with a desire to designate people according to their ages as individuals, but the texts themselves, or the lexicon of childhood used within them, was not equipped for this.

The history of the modern terms *adult, maturation, grow, development* and *metamorphosis* further our sensitivity to this problem. The first came into early-modern English from a French translation of the Latin word *adultus* (to grow-up). Though we have one usage of it in the sixteenth century, before the middle of the seventeenth century (and perhaps a century later) English-speakers typically did not have the noun *adult* in their vocabulary.[41] The levelling implication of the word *adulthood*, as twenty-first-century speakers define it as an internal, universal (perhaps sex-specific) outcome of maturation and experience, does not appear prominently in the medieval knowledge of personhood. A forerunner of *mature* came into English in the early fourteenth century (*maturate*) as an Anglo-Norman word for coming to fruition, and was used in reference to everything from a pustule of infection to fruit, cheese, wine, and other things that ripen. *Mature* becomes a term of personhood no earlier than the seventeenth century and, as with *adult*, its contemporary sense takes a few centuries to unfold. The useful word *maturity* was introduced into English quite specifically as a result of the rise of northern humanists' courtly advice literature. Thomas Elyot's *The Book Named Governour* (1531), the first book of this type written in English, apologized for introducing a "strange and dark" neologism – "maturity".[42]

Elyot needed the new word precisely because there was a poverty of terms in English by which to conceptualize the cultivation of virtue among English nobility.[43] Humanism may have provided a precursor to what moderns call *child development*, but the word *develop* (as we mean it) did not exist. Its roots came into English as *disvelop* from French (*desveloper*) and meant to unfold, unwrap, unroll – as in a map or a flag – such that the contents hidden within could be seen. The medieval body was not a mechanism carrying the blueprint and tools for its own construction. According to Georges Duby, the body was a "sign" of the "soul [that] showed through its envelope of flesh". Its structures ran parallel to the hierarchy of spaces within the monastery, the aristocratic palace. The noble regions were walled-off by the diaphragm from the nether regions so rebellion and desire could be put under sovereign power.[44]

To develop did not become a process (*development*) situated within organisms, and particularly not within human beings until the construction of modern biology. In the nineteenth century, the word *development* (in the sense of persons) helped articulate a distinction between two neologisms: *ontogeny* (development within an organism) and *phylogeny* (evolutionary change within a species). The word played a similar role earlier for the discussion of economic progress.[45] If *development* did not exist in English prior to modern thought, the Anglo-Saxon *weaxan* (to grow) and less frequently *grówan* (to grow), and Middle English *grouen* (*to grow*) all carried the sense of change. *Weaxan* was used most to indicate increasing size and vigour of plants, and secondly to a person's bodily growth of hair, nails and limbs. *Grow* has etymological roots with Germanic terms for grass (O.G. *grô*) and blow (O.E. *blówan* – to blossom or flourish). As it remains today, these terms were better suited to express the concept of external changes in size (quantitative change), than our understanding of development as qualitative change.

The Middle English *disposicioun* (arrangement, plan or order of things) may be more important than *maturate* or *growe* for understanding the distance of medieval thought from the modern concept of "developmental stage". *Disposicioun* could refer to a condition of existence or a balance of elements (the stars, the humours or Providential will). A proper *disposition* was determined by the logic of anterior correspondence with the larger cosmic or theological design. Alternatively, the Latin *metamorphōsis* from the Greek μεταμόρφωσις (change + form) might have carried a stronger sense of human transformation into the vocabularies of the literate groups of medieval England, but the term was isolated to Ovid's text and used mostly to refer to extraordinary or supernatural events of external power such as when Gods turned humans into animals.[46]

If internal transformation did not determine the meaning of human capacity for change, what did? A number of historians argue that the rites of confirmation and marriage marked the transition from child to youth to adult during the Middle Ages. According to Janet Nelson the rite of

DOI: 10.1057/9781137364791

Christian initiation (confirmation) was relocated during the Middle Ages from early childhood to youth because it displaced male haircutting rituals that previously marked coming of age. She suggests that these shifts in youth passages allowed confirmation to serve as a precursor to the marriage-rite as a passage to adulthood.[47] Keith Thomas called confirmation, a rite "marking the arrival of 'social' puberty".[48] Consistent with this line of thought, Jeremy Goldberg has argued that the institution of marriage approximated "social adulthood" in late-medieval England.[49] Barbara Hanawalt likewise stated that those who never married, and lived without substantial holdings, fell "short of full adulthood".[50] In a situation where most people did not need to know their precise date of birth, John Burrow concluded, they marked life-cycle status "by *rites of passage* such as marriage".[51]

In different ways, Burrow, Nelson, Thomas, Goldberg and Hanawalt constructed a path toward "adulthood" for the Middle Ages to make our sense of it more familiar. There is much to be said for the correspondence they imagine. Recall that among commoners during the later Middle Ages, those possessing a competent amount of property were more likely to achieve marriage (Goldberg's *social adulthood*) than those with little or none.[52] Marriage and land rights were interdependent sources of legitimate power for common people across Europe. Working with early-modern Belgian representations, Sandra Hindman called marriage "the principal ritual" of passage from childhood to adulthood.[53] Phyllis Gaffney pointed out that the Old French *enfes* or *enfant* (descendent, heir, rising generation) was not a "span of years", because it could be variously used to name anyone from birth to about age 30, with two centenarians so named. *Enfes* named men who are not responsible for others. It denoted not age, but "a social situation", and was "never" used to refer to a landholder or someone who was married.[54] Doris Berkvam concurs, "age never seems to be an essential factor" in determining adulthood in medieval French literature.[55]

So too, the three word-complexes that framed the discourse of master-servant childhood in English are consistent with Goldberg's idea of "social adulthood". Recall, for example, that the words separating girlhood from womanhood turned around sexual relations made legitimate by marriage; while the words distinguishing boyhood and manhood were invoked around property ownership that made a male eligible to marry. It is reasonable to say that the authority enjoyed by those who married and formed households stood as a pillar of order in medieval

DOI: 10.1057/9781137364791

and early-modern England. Marriage and householding helped constitute the political system in a way that corresponds to the modern liberal
granting of individual rights to competent adults.

Yet there are limitations that come with the phrase "social adulthood". It inserts the child-adult dualism where it does not belong. The
discourse of marriage and householding in Anglo-Saxon, Middle, and
early-modern English was not one of self-possession. This discontinu-
ity should not be glossed over with a social scientific category of "the
social". The rights of possessing a competent household founded upon
the practices and language of patriarchal master-servant relations are
distinct from the rights of possessing a competent self based on the
idea of maturation into adulthood. The concepts of rights, household,
and self are qualitatively different between these two historical frame-
works. As we have seen, the discursive and institutional position of
married, property-holding men of medieval and early modern England
(Goldberg's most complete *social adults*) could not be represented
or practiced without corresponding positions of servitude. These
persons are named collectively as the householder's *maynpast* – an
Anglo-Norman word for his dependents formed out of Latin words for
"hand" and "to feed". To exist a *master, father, husband* needed *boys* or
lads serving the household, *apprentices* learning the mysteries of a craft,
maids and *damsels* performing a variety of tasks under a *wife* working
alongside him, helping manage the house, and bringing forth legitimate
children, sons and *daughters*.[56] The terms of medieval or early-modern
childhood or youth are inseparable from a larger apparatus of servitude
and household production, and these simply are not the processes of
maturation or adulthood. To understand English childhood during the
Middle Ages is to know that it is not the opposite of adulthood, because
the latter did not exist.

Unlike "social adulthood", the phrase *master-servant childhood* avoids
the ahistorical properties of "the social", because it is drawn from the
vocabulary of the period that it is trying to capture. The word *master*
comes from an early Anglo-Saxon word (*mægster*) reinforced by Anglo-
Norman and Middle French terms (*maistre*) which share the same Latin
root (*magister*) initially referring to a male in authority, particularly
teaching authority. Its oldest English uses applied to learned men with
disciples, but it subsequently named other men taking servants to work
within their households, shops and lands. Its female counterpart, *mis-
tress*, comes from the French feminine-form of the word and likewise

DOI: 10.1057/9781137364791

carried the connotations of authority, possessing, teaching and knowing (before it became a synonym for sexual consort).

From the later Middle Ages, but increasingly in the early-modern period, the high title *master* was seized by ordinary English householders and craftsmen – mere *husbands*. Beginning in the sixteenth century, the word *mister* (a Middle English noun for a service or an occupation) began to take from *master* the task of denoting men without higher titles – gentlemen and lower commoners. By the late eighteenth century, any adult male could be addressed with the polite democratic *mister*. The leveling sense of the word reached its full extent with the American debate over the courtesy – *Mr. President.*[57] While *mister* surged toward its democratic purpose, the political position of propertied young males declined. For the first time they were seen as not being "old enough" to wield the rights of common men.[58] Now they might be endearingly called *master* with a first name attached (*master Jack*). At this moment of reversal, when the relations of age became more important than the relations of property for the naming of persons – when English speakers felt that even the diminished word *mister* was not diminutive enough to refer to middle-class boys or young aristocrats, the English language was well on its age-graded journey out of the master-servant mode of thought and feeling. So, the mundane semantic history of *master* and *mister* condenses an amazing historical inversion within English cultures. A fuller comprehension of this reversal in our sense of being and becoming in time (age) requires that we dig more broadly and deeper into European cultural history.

Notes

1   Hilding Back, *The Synonyms for 'Child,' 'Boy,' 'Girl' in Old English: An Etymological-Semasiological Investigation* (Liechtenstein: C.W.K. Gleerup, Lund, 1934): 38–41.

2   See DOE, MED, OED, and Back, *The Synonyms*,1, 52–53, 64–71, 90–98.

3   Albert Keiser, "The Influence of Christianity on the Vocabulary of Old English Poetry," *University of Illinois Studies in Language and Literature* vol. 5, no. 1 (February 1919): 83–84.
    Back, *Synonyms*, 132–134, 144–145.

4   Unless otherwise cited, the Old English Gospels used are from R.M. Liuzza ed., *The Old English Version of the Gospels: Volume One – Text and Introduction* (Oxford: Oxford University Press, 1994): 187; Joseph Bosworth (ed.), *The*

DOI: 10.1057/9781137364791

Gothic and Anglo-Saxon Gospels in Parallel Columns with The Versions of Wycliffe and Tyndale (London: Reeves & Turner, 1888): 526; As cited in the DOE, John 13:33 (Cambridge, Corpus Christi College, MS. 140): Skeat, 1871–1887, 12–186; Skeat, W.W., *The Four Gospels in Anglo-Saxon, Northumbrian, and Old Mercian Versions* (Cambridge) [repr. Darmstadt 1970].

5   Benjamin Thorpe, *The Homilies of the Anglo-Saxon Church Containing the Sermones Catholici, or Homilies of Ælfric, in the Original Anglo-Saxon, with an English Version Volume I.* (London: Ælfric Society, 1844–1846): 278–279.

6   Joseph Bosworth, *An Anglo-Saxon Dictionary, based on the Manuscript Collections* edited and enlarged by T. North Cote Toller (Oxford: Clarendon Press, 2009): 65–66; Back, *The Synonyms*, 3–8, 13, 29, 32–33, 35.

7   Back, *The Synonyms*, 11, 39–40, 38, 54.

8   Back, *The Synonyms*, 45–47, 71–77, 106–108.

9   Matthew 2: 18.

10   Matthew 11:11. *Wifa bearnum* signifies him among all generations, rather than merely in terms begin special among a particular age-group, because other terms are used in the Anglo-Saxon to speak of fetuses or babies as being in a certain state of growth. See Luke 1: 5–18; 2: 23, 34, 40, 43; Matthew 21: 15, 16.

11   Luke 14: 26–27 and Mark 10:29–30.

12   The only complications are six places where *bearn* is part of a compound word, or where words like *generacioun, kynde, seed* or *sones of God* retain the sense of lineage. See John 4:12; 8:37, 39; 11:52; 13:33; 17:12; Matthew 2:18; 3:9; 5:9, 38; 9:2; 12:27; 13:15, 38; 16:2, 17; 17:26; 19:29; 22: 24; 23:31; 27:25; Luke 1:7; 3:8; 5:34; 6:35; 10:6; 13: 28, 34; 17:8; 18:29; 19:44; 20: 34; Mark 3:17; 12:19; 13:12.

13   Margaret Pelling, "Apprenticeship, Health, and Social Cohesion in Early Modern London," *History Workshop Journal* no. 37 (1994): 34.

14   The point is acknowledged in Back, *The Synonyms*, 51, 61.

15   Also see Mark 10: 13–15; Luke 18:16; Matthew 11:25.

16   Bosworth (ed.), *The Gothic and Anglo-Saxon Gospels*, 90–91.

17   Searchable versions of Coverdale's Bible (1535) and Tyndale's New Testament translation (1525) are available at http://www.studylight.org. The Greek υιοθεσία was translated as "childshippe" by Coverdale in Rom 8:23; Rom 9:4; Gal 4:5; in Eph 1:5 he used the phrase "receave us as children". In Wycliffe the term was rendered as "adopcioun of sones" or "adopcioun of Goddis sonys".

18   Back, *Synonyms*, 23–27; Keiser, "The Influence of Christianity on The Vocabulary of Old English Poetry," 31, 83–84.

19   The OED holds that Coverdale invented the term for the purposes of this translation. Coverdale worked from German Bibles and in English especially used Tyndale's New Testament. Tyndale had translated Paul's υιοθεσία several ways: "adopcion", or parenthetically keeping the Latin (adopcio), and with the phrase "receave the inheritauce yt belongeth vnto the naturall sonnes".

DOI: 10.1057/9781137364791

20   Gal 4:5 as given in Geneva (1560) and KJV (1611).

21   Edward James, "Childhood and Youth in the Early Middle Ages," in *Youth in the Middle Ages* edited by P.J.P. Goldberg and Felicity Riddy (Woodbridge, UK: York Medieval Press, 2004): 16.

22   Rom 8: 17 Coverdale (1535).

23   Phyllis Gaffney, *Constructions of Childhood and Youth in Old French Narrative* (Burlington, VT: Ashgate, 2011): 25.

24   Nicholas Orme, "The Culture of Children in Medieval England," *Past & Present* no. 148 (August 1995): 52.

25   William Tyndale, *Expositions and Notes on Sundry Portions of the Holy Scriptures – Together with the Practice of Prelates* edited by Henry Walter (Cambridge, UK: Cambridge University Press, 1849): 214–215.

26   Keith Thomas, *Religion and the Decline of Magic* (New York, NY: Scribner, 1971): 46–53, 70.

27   Thomas, *Religion and the Decline of Magic*, 70–72.

28   Quentin Skinner, *The Foundations of Modern Political Thought – Volume Two: The Age of Reformation* (Cambridge University Press, 1978): 189–238.

29   Thomas, *Religion and the Decline of Magic*, 86.

30   Gaffney, *Constructions of Childhood and Youth*, 7, 27.

31   Nicholas Orme, *Medieval Children* (New Haven, CN: Yale University Press, 2001): 166–167.

32   Sandra Hindman, "Pieter Bruegel's Children's Games, Folly, and Chance," *The Art Bulletin* vol. 63, no. 3 (September 1981): 447–475.

33   *Proverbs* 20:29 (Wycliffe).

34   As quoted in Gaffney, *Constructions of Childhood and Youth*, 37–38.

35   This point is made well by James, "Childhood and Youth in the Early Middle Ages," 14–15, 23.

36   Granville Stanley Hall, *Adolescence; Its Psychology and Its Relations to Physiology, Anthropology, Sociology, Sex, Crime, Religion and Education* (New York, NY: Appleton and Company, 1905).

37   Marc Kleijwegt, *Ancient Youth: The Ambiguity of Youth and the Absence of Adolescence in Greco-Roman Society* (Amsterdam, NL: J.C. Gieben, 1991); James Schultz, *The Knowledge of Childhood in the German Middle Ages, 1100–1350* (Philadelphia, PA: University of Pennsylvania Press, 1995): 39–40.

38   Back, *Synonyms*, 182; Willem Frijhoff, "Historians Discovery of Childhood," *Paedagogica Historica* vol.48, no. 1 (February 2012): 11–29.

39   See the DOE; Back, Synonyms, 167. See Matt 14, 19, 20, 22, 51; Luke 7, 14.

40   John Boswell, *The Kindness of Strangers: The Abandonment of Children in Western Europe from Late Antiquity to the Renaissance* (New York: Pantheon Books, 1988): 27.

41   This is the OED's conclusion.

DOI: 10.1057/9781137364791

42 Robert McCrum, William Cran, and Robert McNeil, *The Story of English* (London, UK: Faber and Faber, 1986): 93.

43 On the mirror-for-princes literature see Quentin Skinner, *The Foundation of Modern Political Thought -- Volume One: The Renaissance* (Cambridge: Cambridge University Press, 1978): 213–243.

44 Georges Duby, "Solitude: Eleventh to Thirteenth Century," in *A History of Private Life: Revelations of the Medieval World -- Volume II* edited by Georges Duby, trans. Arthur Goldhammer (Cambridge MA: The Belknap Press of Harvard University Press, 1988): 522–524.

45 Raymond Williams, *Keywords: A Vocabulary of Culture and Society* revised edition (New York, NY: Oxford University Press, 1983): 102–104, 161–165.

46 See the OED and MED.

47 Janet Nelson, "Parents, Children, and Church in the Earlier Middle Ages," in *The Church and Childhood* edited by Diane Wood (Oxford, UK: Blackwell Publishers, 1994): 99.

48 Thomas, *Religion and the Decline of Magic*, 65.

49 P.J.P. Goldberg, *Medieval England: A Social History, 1250–1550* (New York, NY: Oxford University Press, 2004), 96; also see his outline of the concept in "Masters and Men in Later Medieval England," in *Masculinity in Medieval Europe* edited by D.M. Hadley (New York, NY: Longman, 1999), 56–70.

50 Barbara Hanawalt, *Growing Up in Medieval London: The Experience of Childhood in History* (New York, NY: Oxford University Press, 1993), 174.

51 John Anthony Burrow, *The Ages of Man: A Study in Medieval Writing and Thought* (New York, NY: Oxford University Press, 1988): 93.

52 Orme, *Medieval Children*, 55.

53 Hindman, "Pieter Bruegel's Children's Games, Folly, and Chance," 462.

54 Gaffney, *Constructions of Childhood and Youth*, 26, 30, see note 31.

55 Doris Desclais Berkvam, "Nature and Norrture: A Notion of Medieval Childhood Education," *Mediaevalia* vol. 9 (1983): 168.

56 See Schultz, *The Knowledge of Childhood*, 40–42, 256–259; P.J.P. Goldberg and Felicity Riddy, eds, *Youth in the Middle Ages* (Woodbridge, UK: York Medieval Press, 2004): 5–6.

57 Gordon Wood, *Revolutionary Characters: What Made the Founders Different* (New York: Penguin Books): 54.

58 Holly Brewer, *By Birth or Consent: Children, Law, and the Anglo-American Revolution in Authority* (Chapel Hill, NC: University of North Carolina Press, 2005).

DOI: 10.1057/9781137364791

4

Generation, Age and the Logic of Correspondence

Abstract: *This section takes aim at the ill-conceived idea that "emotional distance" from children was a coping strategy dictated by high child-mortality environments. Our confrontation with the precariousness of our existence cannot be understood with ahistorical psycho-dynamic theories. For the Middle Ages, it requires that we unpack the logic of correspondence that defined the unique position of childhood relative to human mortality in ordinary existence and our capacity for adoption as "children of God". We explore this theme through the complex semantic histories of* generation *and* age, *by examining the Greek sense of* paideia, *and presenting the ancient motif of the Ages of Man.*

Ryan, Patrick Joseph. *Master-Servant Childhood: A History of the Idea of Childhood in Medieval English Culture.* Basingstoke: Palgrave Macmillan, 2013. DOI: 10.1057/9781137364791.

 DOI: 10.1057/9781137364791

The previous section showed that terms most closely associated with *childhood* in English occupied a paradoxical position during the Middle Ages. They were words of growth, earthly impermanence and the profane body; while they provided some of the strongest images for thinking about the human capacity for communion with the eternal order of things – with God. This seeming contradiction cannot be fully explained without dealing with *generation, age* and the medieval double-sense of time as a correspondence between the ordinary and the eternal. Yet first, this section will show that the psycho-dynamic argument that high-mortality necessitated a "defense mechanism" of "emotional distance" from children leads us away from understanding master-servant sensibilities. This section and the next will provide a historically grounded alternative for understanding how medieval Europeans made sense of the precariousness of being and becoming human, and it will locate it in their sense of time.

The discourse of master-servant childhood carried with it a strong sense of generational responsibility, care and family devotion. It simply did not share the modern dualism between power and love, or the opposition between violence and empathy. Little can be said for reading into the ancient or medieval texts a romantic polarity between sentimental parental care/affection and matters of power and property. This does not mean children and childhood were unimportant prior to the modern world.[1] We have Cicero (106–43 BC) supporting the paternal right of exposing deformed newborns as written in *The Twelve Tables*, asking rhetorically, "What is sweeter to man than his children?"[2] With the well-documented Greco-Roman willingness to discard disabled babies, we find that pre-Christian Roman tombs repeatedly offer epitaphs of loss for dearly departed, very young, children. In Publius Papinius Statius' (45–96 AD) *Silvae* a poem "On the Death of a Child" offered: "Shall I not mourn thee, darling boy? with whom,/Childless I missed not children of my own;/I, who first caught and pressed thee to my breast,/and called thee mine, and taught thee sounds and words."[3]

So too, Plato's and Aristotle's support for ridding the polis of deformed newborns was not based upon a rejection of the humanity of children in general, anymore than the contemporary debate over abortion is neatly divided between murderers and saviours of the child.[4] Armed as we are with prenatal testing and hygienic abortive technologies, perhaps we should not be so superior when we consider the Roman *susceptio* – the father's power to accept or reject a newborn's entrance into his house. An

DOI: 10.1057/9781137364791

honest look into current trends toward "screening" (a telling word) for Down's syndrome *in utero* should complicate our moral assessment of the Spartan "leskhe", a council of elders, who had the power to inspect infant boys and remand those deemed defective to the "apthetai", a pit where babies died by exposure or were consumed by wild dogs.[5]

The conditions under which it was legal to expose unwanted children were more restrictive in the Roman Republic than they had been in the Greek *polis*. Yet, Tacitus, Cicero and Plutarch all supported policies of infanticide. In Paul Veyne's estimation, a wide assortment of emotions might describe parent-child relations in pagan Rome, but the "prevailing morality" encouraged fathers to love their children as carriers of the family's name. Infants were abandoned for supremely pragmatic household reasons: deformity at birth, inability to feed the child, a fear that the family could not properly educate the child, a desire to consolidate household resources for the education or inheritance of older siblings. The Romans did not speak of "having" a child, but of "getting" one and "raising" one.[6] Latin terms such as *delicia* for a child purchased as a pet to play with a patrician child, or the use of the term *res vacantes* to refer to orphans, communicates to us volumes about the standing of poor or abandoned children prior to Christianity. These terms also indicate that the position of children was not defined by age-grouping, nearly as much as it was determined by their household relationships.

Hebrew and Christian writers roundly rejected Greco-Roman infanticide, and the spread of their ideas entailed a refashioning of the doctrine of *patria potestas* (the father's dominion over the family) in terms of a pastoral responsibility to care for each and all. The long-term significance of this for ordinary children is probably difficult to overstate. The Hellenistic Jewish scholar, Philo (20 BC–50 AD), seems to have been the first writer to condemn infanticide in Greco-Roman cultures.[7] The reforms of Emperor Hadrian during the next century revoked the paternal right of abandonment. Buying and selling children for immoral purposes was prohibited. The Church Fathers, Justin the Martyr (100–165) and Clement of Alexandria (c. 150–215), harshly attacked practices of infant exposure because they feared it might result in unknown incest if the infant was saved by a neighbouring family.[8] Augustine of Hippo (354–430) taught that it was "not possible to create a superfluous man", but he also asked "who would not choose to die" if salvation meant living in a state of infancy. Pope Leo the Great (c. 391–461) summed-up the Gospel writers' positions on children with the phrase, "Christ loves

DOI: 10.1057/9781137364791

Childhood" for its humility and innocence. Of course, the Church fostered alternative same-sex communities for men and women which provided a life-course outside familial patriarchy, as well as institutional support for children outside of households.[9] The relationship between Christianity and childhood is complex, but clearly it was part of a movement toward a stronger and more all-encompassing ethic of care for the weak and the poor.[10]

If we pause here at the pastoral heart of late-antiquity, as it laid a foundation for the terms of master-servant childhood during the Middle Ages, it is worth recalling how far removed we are from Lloyd deMause's slogan of emancipation that childhood was a nightmare from which we have only recently begun to awaken. The deep structure of childhood is far more ambiguous. We have Anglo-Saxon skeletal remains of persons born with disabilities who survived as long as they did only because someone cared intensely and worked dutifully for them.[11] Nevertheless, these same early medieval sites contain only about one-third of the number of buried children that mortality estimates would project. This may suggest a pattern of unceremonious disposing of children's bodies and would be consistent with the legal acceptance of infanticide among pre-Christianized European tribal groups. Children, especially girls, are notably under-represented in surviving medieval texts, even manorial surveys designed to count everyone and everything.[12] So too, we have evidence from the later medieval period that a large proportion of children under the age of one died in fires. Many may have perished as the lay unattended next to the hearth.[13]

Yet none of this simplifies the mystery of death. This is not due to evidentiary issues, but because human emotion and our profound capacity for loss cannot be numbered on a scale. Love cannot be entirely accounted, spent or withheld, even in a modern market society. Consider the widespread ancient Germanic practice of *wergild*, a system of fines due to a family for a wrongful injury or death. Such a practice seems to suggest the attachment of value to children, even babies. *Wergild* attempted to rectify wrongful damages incurred by parents, children and other kin, and to heal estrangement among powerful groups. The Anglo-Saxons codified rules of *wergild*, weighting the compensation by social status.[14] David Herlihy reported that a seventh-century code among the Visigoths awarded a death benefit of 60 gold coins or sceat as compensation for the wrongful death of a free baby in the first year of life. The fine for killing an infant among

DOI: 10.1057/9781137364791

the Visigoths was substantial, and this suggests an awareness that no house could survive without them. This fine increased on average about four coins per year to 90 coins by age ten years. Between 10 and 15 years the specified compensation increased about 10 coins per year, and it advanced by 30 coins per year between 15 and 20 years old. Between 20 and 50 years old, the *wergild* for men stood at 300 gold coins (or five times the fine for causing a male newborn's death). It declined in old age, returning to the value of a 10-year-old at age 65 and over. This pricing of family losses by age among the early medieval Visigoths makes sense if their code was designed to allow patriarchal households to preserve lineage, labour relations and political legitimacy.[15] Of course, one need not conclude that *wergild* captured all that was felt or thought.

Household-centred assumptions about the importance of persons are a very strong thread in the fabric of master-servant childhood. The Anglo-Saxon legal codes of Ine and Ælfred provided a series of protection for children who lost parents or were otherwise harmed. Generational relations were valued mostly in terms of kinship and inheritance. Because of this, these rules did little to protect young slaves, disabled children and anyone deemed illegitimate. Those without fathers or households, or those unfit to be heirs, had few sources of protection in law.[16] As with *wergild*, the logic of these codes (though demonstrating an awareness of age differences) supported the rights of descent and household membership. It seems to me these political and economic rules demonstrate an attempt to order, to equate, to account for losses felt rather than the absence of such emotions. They demonstrate a concern for children in terms of the predominant hierarchies.

The High Middle Ages brought discoveries and developments that seem to have offered a wider scope for attending to and caring for children.[17] Market towns helped establish independent sources of power for merchant and craft guilds, encouraged an expansion of apprenticeship, and a stronger setting for specialized training of the laity. Georges Duby notes that words for "to earn", became more common, money was used more widely, keys are found in archeological sites more frequently, and settlement expanded beyond the control of the Great Houses. If earlier in the Middle Ages, the "monastery was the mouth of the people", the later medieval centuries saw an advancement of ordinary parish clergy and the invention of the marriage sacrament that resulted in "greater prominence for the [common]

DOI: 10.1057/9781137364791

household, not for the individual". For, "a long time the individual remained the prisoner of the family".[18]

Yet, greater attention to the details of childhood become visible from the eleventh through the thirteenth centuries. Medical knowledge about infancy and early childhood was recovered from Muslim and Greco-Roman texts. There was a striking improvement in the representation of babies and children in what moderns call "developmentally realistic" ways.[19] Thomas Aquinas completed a theological reconfiguration of a harsh Augustinian understanding of the disposition of unbaptized infants' souls. They were not damned to eternal suffering, but were *limbus puerorum* – preserved in a state between heaven and hell. There was a complementary emergence of a "cult of the Christ child". Visions of Jesus as a baby appeared to saints. An existing apocryphal literature and renewed dramatizations of the young Christ's humanity fed a fascination unmet by the Gospels.[20] Monasteries shifted away from taking quite young boys, and preferred that they delay the rigor of monastic discipline until they were youths or young men. There was also a late-medieval, Renaissance-era growth in foundling hospitals and orphanages that cared for the most vulnerable.[21]

In *The American Historical Review*, Alex Novikoff recently outlined the standard theory that the increasing humanism of the twelfth and thirteenth centuries was fostered by a rediscovery of Aristotle and a renewed culture of "scholastic disputation".[22] Scholasticism injected a new subtlety into the discussion of how a person might become virtuous, both in the Christian sense of conversion and the Greek sense of *paideia*.[23] For our purposes, it should be noted that scholasticism and the associated late-medieval institutional developments were entirely consistent with the discourse of master-servant childhood. As Aristotle put it, "children are a good possessed by both parents in common, and a common property holds people together."[24] The ancient understanding that, "by nature... ancestors rule over their descendants", was a statement indicative of the Aristotelian cosmos.[25] D. Brendan Nagel has shown that the household – not the individual – was the foundation of Greek political order. Greek education "was not an experiment in self-discovery or idiosyncratic personal development... nor [were *nomoi* – the traditions the supported the Greek patriarchal sense of virtue] up for discussion or debate."[26]

For the Greeks, learning civic virtue depended upon a correspondence between master-servant households (*oikoi*) and the vitality of a city's

DOI: 10.1057/9781137364791

(*poleis*) festivals and rituals. It was premised on the ideal of freedom from labour (*scholé*) – a word from which we have derived a very different concept of a "school". Only a class possessing *scholé* (leisure) and in command of *oikoi* could pursue virtue and offer magnificent gifts to the public (*euergetism*).[27] Lesser men must pursue self-interest. Fostering virtue through leisure (*paideia*) was antithetical to the work (*ascholé*) conducted by farmers, craftsmen or merchants.[28] The souls of ordinary husbands (much less anyone else) did not merit serious reflection. The classical patriarchy defined by civic virtue and citizenship recognized a decidedly less expansive community than the paternalism that informed the early Middle Ages – framed as it was by ideals of charity, poverty and pastoral care.[29]

The recovery of the discourse of Greek *paideia* for medieval childhood is misconstrued if one reads the term as synonymous with the modern English phrase – 'child-rearing.' Not only was *paideia* restricted to a tiny minority, it was part of a discourse that asked, in Arthur Lovejoy's words, "Why is there any World of Becoming, in addition to the eternal World of Ideas...". The Platonic answer led to a paradox: the supreme essence (the Idea of the Good) in its complete, eternal, absolute fullness entailed the creation of an existence that was incomplete, temporary, changing (the World of Becoming).[30] *Paideia* (becoming virtuous or resembling the Idea) was not achieved by a schooling in disciplinary technologies; it was not a precarious, minute process of internal identification with normative behavior. It was supposed to bring a correspondence between the mind's mastery over the body and the order of the cosmos. This was possible because the Idea of the Good created a likeness of itself within the soul of Man. As C.F. Goody has recently argued, the ancient conceptualization of becoming or being human assumed epistemological and ontological dimensions are external to the individual as a unit of analysis.[31] Veyne made a complementary observation that for Plato "socialization operate[d] at the level of society as a whole, of the regime, and not at that of the subgroups in which everyone is born and lives his life."[32] For Plato, the demands of *paideia* were rigid; only the highest order of activities advanced the mastery of the mind over the body. *Scholé* (leisure) should be restricted to learned discussions, disputations, and lecture groups. He dismisses music, drama, festival, and ritual as unnecessary, even dangerous. Likewise, he urged the republic to eliminate its constituent *oikoi* (household, house, family) altogether to subordinate matters of the flesh. The connections between these arguments and the Christian

DOI: 10.1057/9781137364791

notion of the *imago Dei* and the development of monastic orders from late-antiquity and the Middle Ages have been well documented.[33]

The Platonic idea that all things have their corresponding places informs Aristotle as well. But Aristotle differed sharply with his teacher's propensity to ignore existing conditions, and departed from a wooden compartmentalization of the human subject. Aristotle defended household rituals and city festivals, and argued that virtue could be learned (*paideia*) through music, drama and the arts. As a result, he developed a more flexible, internal sense of human subjectivity. He argued that *mimesis* (the representation of the world through the arts – as opposed to *diegesis* – the telling of a story or a disputation over an issue) could be a powerful force for fostering virtue. The arts created an impression upon the soul, and therefore might establish a proper resemblance or alignment between the essence of things and our temporary existence.[34]

The contrast between Platonic and Aristotelian *paideia* is consistent with Novikoff's conclusion that the rediscovery and translation of Aristotle's writings enlivened medieval schoolmen's discourse on human subjectivity. We might even wonder if the reception of the Aristotelian defence of *mimesis* in the late twelfth century was made ready by earlier developments, such as St. Anselm's (1033–1109) argument that men could come to knowledge of God via the impression of perfection He has left upon the human mind.[35] Yet, the scholastic expansion of interest in human subjectivity, much like Anselm's ontological proof that we can know God exists because we are impressed with Him, should not be equated with a modern sense of the sovereign individual or individuality. We should handle subjectivity with care following Caroline Walker Bynum's qualified, but essentially negative, response to the question, "Did the Twelfth Century Discover the Individual?" Certainly, an interest in the mystery of the inner man was revived in the High Middle Ages, but it confirmed the logic of cosmic correspondence in a chain of being. We are all impressed (as if waxed models) with God's image as His permanence leaves a corresponding mark upon our temporal existence.[36]

The medieval scholastic discourse on the human subject was punctuated by a logic of correspondence that cannot be translated into modern terms of developmental socialization, nor did it provoke the counter-discourses that are currently preoccupied with children's authenticity and agency. Here, the history of the term *individual* is telling. The word

DOI: 10.1057/9781137364791

came into late Middle English from the Latin *individualis* (in + dividere) which was used in late-antiquity to translate the Greek *atomos* (not + cuttable). The roots of *individual* are retained in the modern meaning of *indivisible*. In its initial fifteenth-century sense, *individual* was an adjective applied to things that neither could be divided, nor grouped with other things and retain their identity. A married couple and the Trinity were *individuals* in this sense of the term.

During the High Middle Ages, Latin words such as *anima* (soul), *seipsum* (self), and *homo interior* (inner man) became more prevalent and important tools for learned debate. These terms emerged with a renewed emphasis on the soul, so Caroline Walker Bynum argued, as a space within that should be impressed like wax until it corresponded to *imago Dei* (the image of God). If *homo interior* was aligned in parallel with *imago Dei*, the life of the Christian would be one of service to others. We have a sense of an interior self that should resemble or remain in correspondence with God. This was not a subjectivity unique or isolated or inalienable – not *individual* as the idea shifted with the construction of modern theories of childhood. In the medieval world, there was no modern *individual* as "an order of being" with an internal mechanism fit for analysis. In Raymond Williams' view, making the *individual* into a thing to be explored in its own right (child or adult) required an elaboration of thought from Hobbes's contract to Leibniz's monads to Adam Smith's *employed individual*. Finally, Darwinians helped us think in terms of *developing individuals* within an evolving population.[37] Sprinkle in novel practices of graphic visualization and advancements in statistical reasoning during the twentieth century, and you have the materials for the contemporary medical discourse of childhood entirely free from the logic of correspondence.

The scholastic interest in the human subject does not seem to have inhibited the strength of master-servant assumptions, nor did it provide an alternative to the logic of correspondence from the late-medieval into the early-modern periods. Take the Latinate Middle English word *gneracioun*, which indicated (1) the action of creating, (2) a lineage of descent, or (3) a kind of person determined by breeding.[38] *Generacione* (*genetivum*, belonging to birth) indicated the act of procreation, but it could also be used to position persons in a line of descent, whether earthly or spiritual. As late as the widely circulated English colonial Jeremiad, *The Day of Doom* (1662), Michael Wigglesworth's (1631–1705) used the terms "chosen generation" and "guileful generation" to refer to the saved and

DOI: 10.1057/9781137364791

the damned at the day of judgment, rather than to indicate age groupings or family lines of earthly origins.[39] Wigglesworth's *generation* grouped souls by election (*adoption*) as "children of God" (*childshippe*) and by access to what he called the "Childrens Bread" – an everlasting place in the house of God.[40] In this Calvinist sense, lineage was predetermined by the Creator. Think of this in contrast to positioning the identity of individuals within a demographic group born in a small span of years, sometimes held in opposition to their own parents – the twentieth century's *generation gap*. These two uses of the word (*chosen generation* and *generation gap*) required different conceptual nets to operate. For those thinking of being human as produced in small packets of time and stages of individual development, the Middle and early-modern English terms are easily misread and equated with incommensurate contemporary phrases such as: *the greatest generation, baby-boomers, the me generation, Gen-X,* or *generation Y.*

The older relational, corresponding sense of *generation, child* and *age* is difficult for moderns to grasp because it relies on a concept of time we have lost. There were many Anglo-Saxon and Middle English words associated with time, but medieval chroniclers did not write numbers with a mind for scientific data. Figures were offered as "a literary art to amaze and appall the reader", with the sheer girth of Roman numerals. As Barbara Tuchman cautioned, "medieval chronology is extremely hard to pin down."[41] The new year had various starting points including Christmas, March 1, March 25 and Easter. The concept of the *regnal year* (dating time by royal ascension to the throne) added a layer of ambiguity that confounds our modern sense of time as a replaceable part. If a date of birth drew comment at all in late-medieval texts, it was not written like the forms of a database would have it (03/14/1967). The era of "age-consciousness" had not arrived.[42] When time of birth was noted, it was often given as a number years marking a feast day, or seasons, or assigned importance for having happened under a particular star or sign of the zodiac.[43]

This way of placing things in time – by drawing relationships between (what seems to us) unrelated events should not be dismissed as a lack of rationality. Lovejoy called it "otherworldliness" and located its origins in the tension between Platonic "eternal Ideas" and the "World of becoming." It seems to me that it has more diverse sources, but making sense of this way of being requires some minimal respect for a double-sense of time as a relationship between the sacred and the secular.[44] *Secular* comes

DOI: 10.1057/9781137364791

into Middle English through French from the Latin *saeculum*. It was associated with the word *sēclum* (meaning "an age" or "a century") and *siecle* (meaning "the world"), but its primary usage distinguished clergy who lived in the world, as opposed to monks who rejected it. Charles Taylor offered the insight that the use of *saeculum* is an index for a profound medieval distinction between "ordinary time" and "higher time". Secular, ordinary time is linear: X happens before Y and Y before Z, so X exists before Z and Z cannot be the cause of X. In contrast, "higher time" (liturgical time, cosmic time, sacred time, God's sense of time) is eternal. Eternity carries the essence of things: it is "gathered time"; simultaneous to all things; perfectly fixed; the alpha and the omega; a time of origins; a "time out of mind".[45]

Secular time orients us toward a discussion of causes; sacred or eternal time toward a search for meaning. Cause and meaning could not be divorced in the medieval mind, and this is why they engaged in a search for signs in places where moderns cannot imagine any meaning beyond the relationships between structure and function. It is fitting that the world's first mechanical clocks were built within a sacred architecture. The first ones were monumental constructions raised with bell towers for several late thirteenth-century English Cathedrals. We can trace the historicity of time with the journey from enormous, fixed medieval bell towers, to the ornate, spring-driven noble chamber-clocks of the Renaissance, to the precise seventeenth-century gentleman's pocket watch, to the eighteenth-century marine chronometer.[46] Our sense of being in time was reconfigured with these inventions as secular time freed itself and devoured what Taylor calls "higher" time. This history provided the ontological foundation for an industrial revolution in time discipline.[47]

The relationships between *childhood, generation, age* and the word *kind* (*kynde*) expose the logic of correspondence between ordinary and higher time. C.S. Lewis persuasively argued that the Germanic *kind* occupied a lexical space similar to the Latin words for being born (*gnasci*); characteristic (*natura*), dutiful (*pius*), and to be of good, and known noble family lineage (*generosus* or *genus*). This ancient sense of *kind* came into Middle English and appears to have served a lexical role similar to the multivalent Greek word φύσις or *phusis* (to grow, becoming, origin, or type).[48]

In the English Bible, *generation* and *kind* allowed speakers to gather a sense of being in communion, and its continuity through time if kept

DOI: 10.1057/9781137364791

alive in cultural memory. Take early-modern translations of the Book of Esther, which concluded with a command that the story be told and retold among the Jews so they might remember how their kin (their *kynde*) survived a plotted genocide in Persia (today celebrated as the feast of Purim). In Coverdale's 1535 translation the instruction read that "childers children" should hear the Book of Esther. In other translations it is given that "generaciouns", "every generation" or "generations and generations" should keep alive the memory of who they are.[49] This could be read simply as something any story teller would add to make their stories important. And so it is. But the lesson of Esther, at least as it appears in early-modern English, posits that knowing who you are can be found anterior to your "self". Such knowledge is produced by the telling of the story about your kind (*kin, ken, kynde*). This is to say that who you are came before you were born and it will live after your death – a claim that assumes a distinction between your existence in secular time, and the essence of a higher, cosmic eternal time. The concluding command in Esther makes no sense if you believe (as moderns do) that every existing person possesses their own essence. As Gabrielle Spiegel has shown in a compelling analysis of liturgical time, it is quite difficult for modern scholars to imagine, to experience this older possibility for being in time.[50] A sense of being need not be bound to individualized selfhood. Those reading Esther were being tutored in the idea that they were bound to an essence of things which preceded and extended outside their existence in ordinary time.

Under master-servant childhood, the *natura* (characteristics) of children as such were not as strongly imagined or perceived as they are for moderns. Children could be distinguish into *kynde*, but a child was not a kind of person. There were no *age-groups* in the modern sense of population subsets. The essence of a young person was understood in terms of their lineage which allowed their *kynde* to exist in the world. Chivalric literature provides many examples of *nature* (the essence of what is) speaking louder than *nurture* in the world (existence that is). The boy of noble birth is raised by peasants or merchants, but his nature (his kind, his lineage) will always win out. He will not stick to base labours, he is drawn to daring deeds of sword-play and knightly adventure. The contrasting position for the girl of noble origins is telling. She may very well learn to work with her hands, with her needle-work, but her nature is manifested by her chastity.[51]

In contrast to medieval chivalric literature, Renaissance humanism advanced the importance of nurture, deportment or learning. Late

DOI: 10.1057/9781137364791

fifteenth, early sixteenth-century conduct advice for princes and courtesy poems for noble service circulated as the print revolution brought civic humanism to the English. This movement advanced the importance of nurture, and contributed to a centuries-long, complex transformation of the meanings and relationships between nature and nurture. For Stephen Greenblatt, important Christian humanists such as Thomas More (1478–1535) were torn in faithfulness to the Aristotelian and Christian cosmos (which defined virtue as a correspondence between ordinary time and eternal order and maintained humanity's centrality to Providential design), while they were being seduced by Epicurean ideas that embraced the bodily senses, affirmed ordinary life, rejected a search for resemblance, and ultimately advanced an atomistic, mechanical view of humanity that displaced our pre-eminence within the cosmos.[52] It is within the historical significance of rising humanist thought that the mundane advice offered by English writers such as More, or William Caxton (1422–1492), or Thomas Elyot (1490–1546) should be read. Elyot's *The Boke named the Gouernour* (1531) was a part of a "mirror-for-princes" literature that extended to English elites the humanist critique of luxury, private gain and court corruption.[53] Virtue for More or Elyot was an alignment with external order, but it also depended upon ordinary practices between masters and students, or masters and apprentices, or other lords and servants.[54]

If one wanted to locate the origins of modern ideas about childhood socialization, one could start with Renaissance humanism; yet it is important to avoid introducing theories of developmental socialization where they do not exist. By analogy, listen to Veyne addressing the difficulty modern scholars have understanding education in classical Rome:

> [It] is a peculiar error to think that schools always perform the same function, that of shaping man or adapting him to society. Roman education was neither formative nor utilitarian ... it conferred prestige. ... the minds of little boys were decked out with rhetoric, much as in the last century the bodies of little boys were decked out with sailor suits or military uniforms.[55]

These distinctions are easily lost. Consider the twentieth-century version of Thomas More's (1478–1535) *Utopia* (orig. pub., Latin, 1516). In modern English, More gives "the chief aim of [Utopia's] institutions and government, above all else, is to give all citizens as much time as public needs permit for freeing and developing their minds."[56] Compare this to the seventeenth-century English translation of the same passage:

DOI: 10.1057/9781137364791

"For why, in the institution of the Weale publike, this end is only and chiefely pretended and minded, that what time may possibly be spared from the necessary occupations and affaires of the Common-wealth, all that the Citizens should withdraw from the bodily service to the free liberty of the minde, and garnishing the same."[57] The early-modern version does not speak of the mind as a developing mechanism, but rather defines it through the opposition between "bodily service" and "free liberty". The seventeenth-century translation located the "felicitie of this life" in "garnishing" the mind (as opposed to the ornaments of bodily luxury).

Here, it is enough to say that Old, Middle and early-modern English was better suited to speak of being human in terms of lineal descent, alignment, correspondence, than in the terms of the modern developing individual. This part of our semantic history leaves its trace whenever we read early-modern sources speaking of someone born of an unmarried woman as "a child of no one", or less sharply when later English-speakers said that a stranger, beggar, slave, or servant was a person "of no family". A master-servant sensibility helped frame the late-medieval poem warning against training servile peasant boys as apprentices: "By olde tyme, wryten Y fynde/That prentes shchulde be of gentyl kynde."[58] The class politics of restricting apprenticeship are plain enough, but here we seek to grasp something subtler about these words than their uses in the struggles to achieve economic dominance. It is more important to see that being of *gentyl kynde* was neither a personality trait, nor a property of the individual.

Medieval institutions that provided access to knowledge (apprenticeship) and legitimated power (lordship) furthered the assumption that the essence of authority followed lines of inheritance rooted in and corresponding to the origin of all things: God. Carole Walker Bynum identified a general thread in this history of ideas when she argued that female mystics of the thirteenth century did not hold a sense of the self that could be grasped in terms of developmental psychology or the slogans of liberalism, but only by understanding a discourse of servitude that attempted to locate the "imago dei" (image of God) stamped upon our collective being.[59] Likewise, the master-servant word complexes helped people imagine that the *essence* (from Latin *esse* to be, L14C; based on the Greek οὐσία) of a cosmic patriarchy preceded and was manifested through the *existence* (from Latin *ex* = out + *stā* = stand, L14C) of generations and children. This was

DOI: 10.1057/9781137364791

exemplified well by the scholastic tradition stemming from Aristotle, reformulated by Aquinas, whereby the essence of things other than God was conceived and determined by God prior to human existence or being human in ordinary time. From a scholastic perspective, *that* particular children came to exist or ceased to exist must unfold in ordinary time, but *what* childhood was in essence could not be an experience or process unfolding within the body.[60] With this ontology in mind, one easily could believe that a newborn was stained with "original" sin (the essence of human failure), prior to having committed "actual" sins of the existing world.[61] None of this implied deprecation of children's worth in a developmental sense.

The generative tension between essence (higher time) and existence (ordinary time) was inherited from ancient discourses, and we find its mark on the most elementary term in Latinate languages for relating being and time: *age*. *Age* came into Middle English from Old French (*aäge, eäge*) with a Latin root (*ætāticum*) as a word for naming a period of existence. From its earliest English uses the word has been strongly associated with the passing of time during a person's life, but it also carried a cosmic dimension handed-down from antiquity under the heading – *ætātes hominum* or *the ages of Man*. *The ages of Man* aligned the changes of ordinary life with a higher sense of historical, astrological, seasonal, spiritual cycles.

The ages of Man is not a particular representation, or even a set of representations. It is a motif that has allowed historians to make sense of a large range of texts and artefacts from baptistery carvings and stained-glass windows, and elaborately sculpted into cathedral walls. We find it in encyclopaedia, medical handbooks, poetics, homiletics, cyclical diagrams or *rota*, and pictorial bibles. It was woven into tapestries, carved into household furniture, and decoratively painted upon the walls of family residences. *The ages of Man* displayed the essence of things by finding anterior correspondences between existing things. It was not a means of explaining existence in terms of internal mechanisms. Whether time was divided into three, four, six, seven ages, the *ages of Man* were premised on the idea that the earth changed in a cyclical pattern, while the heavens sat eternal, perfect, fixed. Experiencing time as a cycle permitted the transience of the human condition to be related to the idea of an eternal order of the divine. It specified the correspondence between the dynamic elements of existence and the eternal essence of the universe.[62] This cyclical sense of being in time

DOI: 10.1057/9781137364791

positioned the human subject as moving parallel to the cosmos, rather than as a unit of analysis containing a mechanism unfolding *within* itself.

The resemblances (*comparationes*) located by *the ages of Man* were initially numerological. The oldest system meditated on the power of the number four, and may have been first articulated by Pythagoras. This served to order the Stoic quadrivium of arithmetic, geometry, music and astronomy.[63] We continue to experience its remnants when we speak of four seasons and see in four directions. Ovid's *Metamorphoses* had Pythagoras ask its readers, " do you not see the year assuming four aspects, in imitation of your own lifetime? For in early Spring it is tender and full of fresh life, just like a little child."[64] Through the medieval period, the Latin terms *pueritia, adolescentia, iuventus, senectus* frequently named the four corresponding cycles of a life. These four ages were preferred by medieval physicians because they fit with humoural theory (phlegm, blood, yellow gall, and black gall).[65] They also assembled the four points of the arch of the Sun used to compute the date of Easter, or to articulate the Cardinal virtues of prudence, justice, temperance and fortitude, which medieval theologians added to the three ancient ones of faith, hope and charity.[66]

The Venerable Bede (672/3–735) was the first Anglo-Saxon known to position the life-cycle within a four-fold cosmic development of time.[67] Many others followed. An early twelfth-century book that may have been written by an Anglo-Saxon, *Tractatus de quarternario*, aligned the four directions, four season, four humours, four elements (earth, wind, fire, and water), four winds, four points of arch of the sun, and four ages of man. To these were added the four letters which spelled the names of both the first man (Adam) and God (Deus).[68] Other writers noted that there were four Gospels, four rivers of paradise, and four historical generations (Adam-Noah, Noah-Abraham, Abraham-Moses, Moses-Jesus). A work once attributed to Bede, *De mundi celestris terrestrisque constitutione* (but now dated three centuries later) captured neatly the corresponding sympathy that aligned humors, seasons, elements of matter, and cycle of life: "Blood resembles air, increases in spring, and dominates in *pureritia* (childhood). Red gall resembles fire, increases in summer, and dominates in *adolescentia* (youth)" and so on. The logic of correspondence as a means for understanding the human body would not come under sustained critique until the seventeenth century.[69]

DOI: 10.1057/9781137364791

The unique prime number seven also served to frame *the ages of Man.* The soul was created by the fixed realm of the stars, passing at birth through the seven planets where it took on the characteristics of their positions, and manifesting this within the life of a person.[70] Four sets of seven days set the lunar cycle, and seven heavenly virtues (and corresponding vices) were established during the middle ages. As the fifth-century Roman African, Macrobius put it, "seven is the number by which man is conceived, developed in the womb, is born, lives and is sustained, and passing through all stages of life attains old age."[71] We continue to live by seven-day weeks, and the Roman seven-year stages of legal responsibility remains in use (especially at three multiples of seven – 21 years) even if the numerology has been forgotten.

The cosmic systems of fours and sevens had pagan origins, but they set the numerological framework for Augustine's influential six-part scheme of time.[72] Augustine's numerology was distinctive because it provided a way of reading texts – a hermeneutic device. He began with Genesis 1–2: six days of creation corresponds to six ages of historical movement, followed by one everlasting day (a seventh heaven) of rest.[73] Augustinians used the number six to read the passage of the wedding at Cana when Jesus transforms the water into wine. The water was the historical sense of time that filled the mind of Man until Christian doctrine transformed it into the spiritual wine of communion with God. The vessels were six in number, because it would take six ages to save the world, just as it took six days to create it. Several centuries after Augustine, the six corresponding Latin terms for the life cycle (*infantia, pueritia, adolescentia, iuventus, gravitas,* and *senectus*) were added to complete the list of correspondences.

One of the earliest visual representations of the numerology of sixes survives upon the stained-glassed windows of Christ Church Cathedral, Canterbury – fashioned in the late twelfth century. The inscription on the window reads, "God here transforms the water of vice into the wine of good ways." Terms naming the six ages of life are inscribed next to images of a baby, a boy with a curved stick and a ball, a light-bearded youth grasping a sceptre, a full-bearded man holding a sword, an aging man with a bag of money, and a balding, white bearded man with a crutch. Corresponding to this we find six figures representing biblical history: Adam, Noah, Abraham, David, Jechonias (last King of Judea prior to the Captivity), and Jesus. The analogue between the transformation of water into wine, the spiritual salvation of humanity, and the growth of persons

DOI: 10.1057/9781137364791

could not be more tightly formed. Pictorial Bibles dating from the next century offered similar representations.[74]

The sixth-century Pope, St Gregory the Great, advanced a five-part cycle of time as a means of biblical interpretation. He began with the observation that there were five books of Moses and five transformations in the nature of the covenant: Eden, the Deluge, the Abrahamic Covenant, Mosaic Law, and the Gospel. These shifts corresponded to childhood, youth, manhood, old age, and death.[75] The five Gregorian divisions of time were used to read the parable of the vineyard (Matthew 20: 1–16), first appearing in a Middle English text in the thirteenth century.[76] The householder (God) called workers (Christians) to the vineyard (the Church) during five hours of the day (five ages of history and five ages of life) with the same payment (salvation) regardless of how early they answered the call.

Another Gregorian way of reading found secret meaning in recurring threes. Three Magi sought the manifestation of God on earth. Beginning in late-antiquity, the three kings were depicted in clothing, skin colour, and by the strength and colour of their facial hair as representatives of the three known continents (Europe, Africa, and Asia) and the three ages of Man (boyhood, manhood, old age).[77] To these three was aligned the parable of the three vigils for the return of the Lord. The periods of waiting were times of conversion assigned to ages of life where they were believed most likely to occur: *pueritia, adolescentia* and *senectus*.[78]

In contrast with the Augustinian equation of childhood with the water of the earth and manhood with conversion to the wine of salvation, Gregorian biblical exegesis by fives and threes offered an affirmative view of children and youths. But this difference should not obscure a more important continuity. Whether following a system of threes, fours, fives, sixes, sevens; whether offered first by Christian or Pagan writers; whether used to read astrological phenomena or biblical text, all the variations upon *The Ages of Man* shared the epistemology of correspondence and resemblance that rested upon a hierarchical relationship between ordinary time and eternal time. They sought to uncover an otherwise hidden order (*logos* or *ratiō*) to earthly being in time and to define the essence of the cycle of life by analog and reversal.

By late-medieval England, *The Ages of Man* had become a familiar device for aligning the human life-cycle with observed astrological phenomena, experienced through seasonal variations, and designed to enhance scriptural memory, as these were all understood to be manifestations of a single

DOI: 10.1057/9781137364791

divine Will. Chaucer's *Knight's Tale*, Gawain-poet's *The Pearl*, and Langland's *Piers Plowman* all drew upon *The Ages of Man*.[79] Arguably its emphasis had shifted toward a more negative view of the "brevity and wretchedness of this life", and this may have been related to a gradual collapse of the logic of correspondence. Certainly, depictions of human aging became less concerned with numerological correspondence. Shaping conduct to conform to the various stages of existence became more important.[80] The shift toward a stronger sense of the human subject may be sensed in this modern English translation of a thirteenth-century poem:

> Of all the months the first behold
> January two-faced and cold
> Because its eyes two ways are cast,
> To face the future and the past.
> Thus the child six summers old
> Is not worth much when all is told
> But one must take every care
> To see that he is fed good fare,
> For he who does not start life well
> Will finish badly, one can tell...
> When October winds do blow,
> Then a man his wheat must sow
> To feed the other men on earth;
> Thus must act a man of worth
> Who has arrived at sixty years:
> He must sow in young folk's ears
> Wisdom all their hearts to fill,
> And give them charity if he will.[81]

The tenderness we hear in this poem may come as much from its twentieth-century English translation, as it does from its late-medieval French source. It speaks to the argument that a sense of mutual responsibilities between the generations has been a point of continuity across many centuries.

Nevertheless, the poem's sense of time as an eternal cycle may strike modern readers as something like a yearning for wholeness. For many, the idea of eternal, liturgical, or sacred time (the correspondence between essence and existence) has been reduced to nostalgia. It no longer provides a governing discursive structure for our civilization. We are separated from the world that gave us *The Ages of Man* by a dominant conceptualization of time as an independent Baconian or Newtonian variable, and by the idea that time can be bought and sold.[82] Prior to the

DOI: 10.1057/9781137364791

collapse of the logic of correspondence, *age* did not (could not) serve as a baseline for examining particular individuals within a population. Psycho-social terms such as *age-group, age-set, age-class, age-distribution, age-grading, age-limit, age-range, age-determination* were all coined in the twentieth century under the force of new types of graphic visualization that extended what Foucault called *normalizing judgment* deeply into the fabric of modern childhood.[83] Conceptualizing this shift in the meaning of *age* requires that we grapple with the word least amenable to analysis in the English language: the verb *to be*.

Notes

1   Beryl Rawson, *Children and Childhood in Roman Italy* (New York, NY: Oxford University Press, 2003).
2   Marcus Tullius Cicero, *The Speeches*. vol. 3, trans. by N.H. Watts (Cambridge, MA: Harvard University Press, 1961): 103.
3   Horace Elisha Scudder, *Childhood in Literature and Art – With Some Observations on Literature for Children: A Study* first published 1894 (New York, NY: Elibron Classics, 2006): 33–34.
4   For Aristotle see book VII, part 16, sec. 15 *The Politics Vol. 1* trans. Benjamin Jowett (Oxford: The Claredon Press, 1885): 240. See book IV, sec. 443c–444e and book V, sec. 461c of *The Republic of Plato* trans. Allan Bloom, 2nd edition (New York, NY: Basic Books, 1991): 123–124, 140. Also see Plato's metaphor between examining and discarding infants and ideas in sec. 149d-e and sec. 160e–161a of *The Theaetetus* trans. F.A. Paley (London: G. Bell, 1875): 15–16, 38.
5   On the abortion of fetuses with disabilities diagnosed in utero see, Caroline Mansfield, Suellen Hopfer, Theresa M. Marteau, "Termination Rates after Prenatal Diagnosis of Down Syndrome, Spina Bifida, Anencephaly, and Turner and Klinefelter Syndromes: A Systematic Literature Review," *Prenatal Diagnosis* vol. 19, no. 9 (September 1999): 808–812.
6   Paul Veyne, "From Mother's Womb to Last Will and Testament," in *A History of Private Life: From Pagan Rome to Byzantium – Volume I* edited by Paul Veyne, trans. by Arthur Goldhammer (The Belknap Press of Harvard University Press, 1987): 9–11, 17.
7   David Herlihy, "Medieval Children," *Essays on Medieval Civilization: The Walter Prescott Webb Memorial Lectures* edited by Bede Karl Lackner and Kenneth Roy Philip (Austin, TX: University of Texas Press, 1978): 113.
8   Angel R. Colon, *A History of Children: A Socio-Cultural Survey across Millennium* (Westport, CN: Greenwood Press, 2001): 68–69, 80–81, 90–92, 94, 104–105; Odd Magne Bakke, *When Children Became People: The Birth of*

DOI: 10.1057/9781137364791

Childhood in Early Christianity trans. by Brian McNeil (Minneapolis, MN: Fortress Press, 2005).

9   Gillian Clark, "The Fathers and the Children," in *The Church and Childhood* edited by Diana Wood (Oxford, UK: Blackwell Publishing, 1994): 5–11, 17–18; Hugh Cunningham, *The Invention of Childhood* (London, UK: BBC Books, 2006): 28–29, 33, 37–39.

10 Paul Veyne, *Bread and Circuses: Historical Sociology and Political Pluralism* trans. by Brian Pearce (New York: Penguin Books, 1990): 19–34.

11 Sally E.E. Crawford, *Childhood in Anglo-Saxon England* (Stroud, Gloucestershire, UK: Sutton Publishing, 1999): 92–101.

12 Herlihy, "Medieval Children," 116–117.

13 Colon, *A History of* Children, 112–114, 226, 235; Elizabeth Coleman, "Infanticide in the Early Middle Ages," in S.M. Stuard (ed.) *Women in Medieval Society* (1976): 47–71.

14 Patrick Wormald, *The Making of English Law: King Alfred to the Twelfth Century* (Oxford, U.K.: Blackwell Publishers, 1999): 374–378; Dorothy Whitelock (ed.), *English Historical Documents- Volume I c. 500–1042* (London, UK: Eyre & Spottiswoode, 1955): 54–55.

15 Herlihy, "Medieval Children," 114–115.

16 Mathew S. Kuefler, "A Wryed Existence: Attitudes Toward Children in Anglo-Saxon England," *Journal of Social History* vol. 24 no. 4 (Summer 1991): 827.

17 Cogently outlined in Herlihy, "Medieval Children," 120–128.

18 Georges Duby, "Solitude: Eleventh to Thirteenth Century," in *A History of Private Life: Revelations of the Medieval World – Volume II* edited by Georges Duby, trans. Arthur Goldhammer (Cambridge MA: The Belknap Press of Harvard University Press, 1988): 511–514, 528.

19 Ariès has been rightly criticized for his handling of iconography, but his sense of a twelfth- or thirteenth-century shift toward "life-like" or "realistic" representation of the human body has not been overturned. The point is stated well by Andrew Martindale in "The Children in the Picture: A Medieval Perspective," in *The Church and Childhood* edited by Diane Wood (Oxford, UK: Blackwell Publishers, 1994): 206. Also see Duby, "Solitude," 512, 524.

20 Mary Dzon, "Joseph and the Amazing Christ-Child of Late-Medieval Legend," in Albrecht Classen (ed.) *Childhood in the Middle Ages and the Renaissance: The Results of a Paradigm Shift in the History of Mentality* (New York, NY: Walter De Gruyter, 2005): 140, 146–147.

21 Nicholas Terpstra, *Abandoned Children of the Italian Renaissance: Orphan Care in Florence and Bologna* (Baltimore, MD: Johns Hopkins University Press, 2005).

22 Alex J. Novikoff, "Toward a Cultural History of Scholastic Disputation," in *American Historical Review* vol. 117, no. 2 (April 2012): 331–364. Also see Colin Morris, *The Discovery of the Individual, 1050–1200* (London, UK: SPCK, 1972).

DOI: 10.1057/9781137364791

23 For a balanced overview of the scholastic contribution to humanism which does not erase the distinction between the two, see Quentin Skinner, *The Foundations of Modern Political Thought – Volume One: The Renaissance* (Cambridge, UK: Cambridge University Press, 1978): 23–65.

24 Aristotle, *Politics*, 1162a 28–29.

25 See William Lambert Newman's assessment in Aristotle's, *Politics* (Oxford: Claredon Press, 1887); Aristotle, *Politics*, 1161a 18–19.

26 D. Brendan Nagle, *The Household as the Foundation of Aristotle's Polis* (Cambridge, UK: Cambridge University Press, 2006): 160; 227–244, 88–91; see also Nagle's helpful discussion of the patterning of deliberative reason and the citizenship on household status, pgs. 103–107, 162, and 196.

27 Veyne, *Bread and Circuses*, xiii, 8–10, 16, 31, 38–40, 45–51,

28 Nagle, *The Household as the Foundation of Aristotle's Polis*, 118–122, 274–275.

29 Veyne, *Bread and Circuses*, 19–33. Foucault formulates this as the contrast between the city-citizenship game and the shepherd-flock game in his 1978 lectures at the College de France, edited by Michel Senelbart, *Security, Territory, Population* trans. Graham Burchell (New York: Palgrave Macmillan, 2009).

30 Arthur O. Lovejoy, *The Great Chain of Being: A Study of the History of an Idea* (Cambridge, MA: Harvard University Press, 1936 and 1964): 45–66.

31 C.F. Goody, *A History of Intelligence and 'Intellectual Disability': The Shaping of Psychology in Early Modern Europe* (Burlington, VT: Ashgate Publishing Company, 2011): 15–39.

32 Veyne, *Bread and Circuses*, 79–80.

33 Lovejoy, *The Great Chain of Being*, 67–98; Gerard O'Daly, *Platonism Pagan and Christian: Studies in Plotinus and Augustine* (Burlington, VT: Ashgate Publishing Company, 2001).

34 Nagle, *The Household as the Foundation of Aristotle's Polis*, 227–289.

35 Richard William Southern, *The Making of the Middle Ages* (New Haven, CN: Yale University Press, 1953): 212–229.

36 Caroline Walker Bynum, "Did the Twelfth Century Discover the Individual?" *Jesus as Mother: Studies in the Spirituality of the High Middle Ages* (Berkeley, CA: University of California Press, 1982): 82–109.

37 Williams, *Keywords: A Vocabulary of Culture and Society* revised edition (New York, NY: Oxford University Press, 1983): 102–104, 161–165.

38 Gen 2:4; Matt 1:11; Psalms 8:6 in Wycliffe (1395); see the earliest know usages in Hans Kurath and Sherman M. Kuhn (eds), *Middle English Dictionary* (Ann Arbor, MI: University of Michigan Press, 1954–2001).

39 Michael Wigglesworth, *The Day of Doom, or a Poetical Description of the Great and Last Judgment, with Other Poems* Orig. publ. 1662, edited by Kenneth B. Murdock (New York: The Spiral Press, 1929): p. 19, sec. 42, p. 30, sec. 84.

40 Wigglesworth, *Day of Doom*, p. 30, sec. 85.

DOI: 10.1057/9781137364791

41   Barbara Tuchman, *A Distant Mirror: The Calamitous 14th Century* (New York, NY: Ballantine Books, 1978): xv–xvi. On Anglo-Saxon words for time see, Janet Bately, "On Some Words for Time in Old English Literature," in *Problems of Old English Lexicography: Studies in Memory of Angus Cameron* edited by Alfred Bammesberger (Regensburg, GDR: Verlag Friedrich Pustet, 1985): 47–64.

42   Howard P. Chudacoff, *How Old Are You? Age Consciousness in American Culture* (Princeton, NJ: Princeton University Press, 1989).

43   Orme, *Medieval Children* (New Haven, CN: Yale University Press, 2001): 45–46.

44   Lovejoy, *The Great Chain of Being*, 24–66, 82–86; Eamon Duffy, *The Stripping of the Alters: Traditional Religion in England, c. 1400–1580* (New Haven, CN: Yale University Press, 1992): 46–52.

45   Charles Taylor, *A Secular Age* (Cambridge, MA: The Belknap Press of Harvard University Press, 2007): 54–61.

46   Samuel Guye and Henri Michel, *Time & Space: Measuring Instruments from the 15th to the 19th Century* (New York, NY: Praeger Publishers,1970).

47   Edward P. Thompson, "Time, Work-Discipline, and Industrial Capitalism," *Past & Present* no. 38 (December 1967): 56–97; David S. Landes, *Revolution in Time: Clocks and the Marking of the Modern World* (Cambridge, MA: Belknap Press of Harvard University Press, 1983).

48   Clive Staples Lewis, *Studies in Words,* 2nd edition (London: Cambridge University Press, 1967): 27; Hilding Back, *The Synonyms for 'Child,' 'Boy,' 'Girl' in Old English: An Etymological-Semasiological Investigation* (Liechtenstein: C.W.K. Gleerup, Lund, 1934): 9; Dominique Barthelemy, "Kinship," in *A History of Private Life – Vol. II – Revelations of the Medieval World* edited by Georges Duby, trans. Arthur Goldhammer (Cambridge, MA: The Belknap Press of Harvard University Press, 1988): 88.

49   Esther 9:28 (Coverdale, 1535); Esther 9:28 (Geneva, 1560).

50   Gabrielle M. Spiegel, "Memory and History: Liturgical Time and Historical Time," *History and Theory* vol. 41 (May 2002): 149–162.

51   Doris Desclais Berkvam, "Nature and Norrture: A Notion of Medieval Childhood Education," *Mediaevalia* vol. 9 (1983): 171.

52   In light of the history of utilitarianism and disciplinary institutions for childhood, my view of Epicureanism is less than celebratory. Yet, its revival seems significant for the modern sensibility. See Stephen Greenblatt, *The Swerve: How the World Became Modern* (New York, NY: WW Norton & Company, 2011): 227–233.

53   Skinner, *The Foundations of Modern Political Thought – volume one*, 228–236, 240–241.

54   Merridee L. Bailey, *Socialising the Child in Late Medieval England*, c. 1400–1600, (Woodbridge, UK: York University Press, 2012): 14–15.

DOI: 10.1057/9781137364791

55 Paul Veyne, "From Mother's Womb to Last Will and Testament," in *A History of Private Life: From Pagan Rome to Byzantium – Volume I* edited by Paul Veyne, trans. by Arthur Goldhammer (The Belknap Press of Harvard University Press, 1987): 20.

56 Thomas More, *Utopia* trans. H.V.S. Ogden (Northbrook, IL: AHM Publishing Corporation, 1949): 33–34.

57 Thomas More, *Utopia* (London: Bernard Alsop, 1624): 54. Accessed [August 24, 2012] *Early English Books Online*, Reel position: STC/1491:05, Henry E. Huntington Library and Art Gallery. Also compare the following passages respectively the above cited translations; (1624): 17–18, 28, 60. 62, 65, 74, 79, and 82; and (1949): 1, 18, 37, 40, 41, 44, and 46.

58 Barbara Hanawalt, *Growing Up in Medieval England: The Experience of Childhood in History* (New York, NY: Oxford University Press, 1993): 145.

59 Caroline Walker Bynum, "Women Mystics in the Thirteenth Century: The Case of the Nuns of Helfta," in *Jesus as Mother: Studies in the Spirituality of the High Middle Ages* (Berkeley, CA: University of California Press, 1982): 170–262.

60 See Thomas Aquinas, *On Being and Existence* (c. 1225?–1274) trans. Armand Maurer (Toronto, Canada: Pontifical Institute of Mediaeval Studies, 1949).

61 See Thomas Aquinas, *Summa Theologica* (New York, NY: Benzinger Brothers, 1947–1948): the first part of the second part, question 82.

62 Elizabeth Sears, *The Ages of Man: Medieval Interpretations of the Life Cycle* (Princeton, NJ: Princeton University Press, 1986): 19, 47–48.

63 Sears, *The Ages of Man*, 9–10.

64 John Anthony Burrow, *The Ages of Man: A Study in Medieval Writing and Thought* (New York, NY: Oxford University Press, 1988): 14.

65 Taylor's comments on correspondence, the humors, and black bile support the larger point; see Taylor, *A Secular Age*, 37–38.

66 Sears, *The Ages of Man*, 17, 20–21.

67 Burrow, *The Ages of Man*, 12–13.

68 Sears, *The Ages of Man*, 23 and figure 6.

69 Keith Thomas, *Religion and the Decline of Magic* (New York, N.Y.: Scribner, 1971): 10–17; Sears, *The Ages of Man*, 21–22, 27.

70 Burrow, *The Ages of Man*, 38–41; Sears, *The Ages of Man*, 38–52.

71 Sears, *The Ages of Man*, 43.

72 Cunningham, *The Invention of Childhood*, 31–32.

73 Sears, *The Ages of Man*, 54–58, 62, 72–74.

74 Burrow, *The Ages of Man*, 90–91.

75 Sears, *The Ages of Man*, 84–88.

76 Burrow, *The Ages of Man*, 63.

77 Burrow, *The Ages of Man*, 136.

78 Sears, *The Ages of Man*, 88–94.

79 Burrow, *The Ages of Man*, 10–11, 30, 40–54, 64–66, 143–146,

DOI: 10.1057/9781137364791

80   Sears, *The Ages of Man*, 98, 113, 120–124, 138–140.

81   Philippe Ariès, *Centuries of Childhood: A Social History of Family Life* trans. by Robert Baldick (New York: Vintage Books, 1962): 22.

82   W.A. Wallace, "Newtonian Antinomies Against the *Prima Via*," *The Thomist: A Speculative Quarterly Review of Theology and Philosophy* vol. 19, no. 2 (April 1956): 151–192; Ian Hacking, *The Emergence of Probability: A Philosophical Study of Early Ideas about Probability, Induction and Statistical Inference* (New York, NY: Cambridge University Press, 1975); Ian Hacking, *The Taming of Chance* (New York, NY: Cambridge University Press, 1990).

83   The epistemological shift is outlined in Michel Foucault, *The Order of Things: An Archaeology of the Human Sciences* (New York, NY: Vintage Books, 1970). In *Discipline and Punish: The Birth of the Prison* trans. Alan Sheridan (New York, NY: Pantheon Books, 1977), Foucault explored the modern episteme in terms of disciplinary techniques of hierarchical observation, normalizing judgment, and the examination. On graphic visualization see Andre Turmel, *A Historical Sociology of Childhood: Developmental Thinking, Categorization, and Graphic Visualization* (Cambridge, UK: Cambridge University Press, 2008).

DOI: 10.1057/9781137364791

5

The Master-Servant Sense of Being in Time

Abstract: Be, being *and* becoming *provide a limit to the analysis of the terms of master-servant childhood because these words make meaning possible by containing none. This is a special problem for the terms of* childhood *because they are all (ultimately) grounded in being. But, this limit is also the great source of childhood's ontological and historical significance. The discursive shifts of childhood over time provide important opportunities for gathering a historical sense of the self, gaining insight into the historicity of being human, and making a historical ontology possible. This section offers explorations in this direction through literary, philosophical, and theological analysis of the* Feast of the Holy Innocents, *the* Boy Bishop, *apocryphal and canonical texts, and the* Lives of Saints, *among other texts – ancient, medieval and modern.*

Ryan, Patrick Joseph. *Master-Servant Childhood: A History of the Idea of Childhood in Medieval English Culture.* Basingstoke: Palgrave Macmillan, 2013. DOI: 10.1057/9781137364791.

If our sense of becoming human transcended language and time, childhood could have no historicity. At best, history would be window dressing for the study of children. On the other hand, if the order of being and becoming human (childhood) has been produced by language and time, its study must be historical. With this, all ontological work on ourselves would have to be historical.[1] Yet we face a serious problem of reading. *Age* (being in time) and its variants stem from the concept spoken by the verb *to be*. Reading *age* historically is especially difficult because the verb *to be* (Anglo-Saxon *beon*; Middle English *bi, bie, bee*) sits like a black box, unable to disclose itself. Unlike all other words, *to be* creates propositional language itself, providing the linguistic foundation for all sensibility. As Foucault put it, *être* (derived from the Latin *esse*) alone is "capable of crossing the frontier of signs and providing them with a foundation in truth".[2] *To be* not only makes possible the networks of meaning that produce truth, it allows them to shift historically; yet this requires that variations of *to be* have no identified position within the network of meaning – at least not ones that can be viewed from within the network itself. *To be* creates meaning because it appears to have none. This opacity makes *to be* seem unchanging – transcendent – when read from within the systems that use it. And, therein lies the heart of the difficulty of reading the child-age-generation word complex, or childhood itself, historically.

The idea that the verb *to be* makes meaning possible, precisely because it cannot disclose its own identity, does not begin with Foucault. Plato's allegory of the cave pictured the problem of human sensibility bound to a field of representation that separates us from a knowledge of our own existence. The same problem is more profoundly expressed in the stories of the Hebrew Pentateuch. The limits of representation speak as the burning bush on Mt Sinai saying for itself only "I *am* that I *am*."[3] Like these ancient sources, Foucault's discussion of *to be* challenges the modern rejection of the limits of representation. Our hubris arrived with a modern faith that our knowledge of the essence of things could be liberated from the obscurity of the burning bush by scientific techniques of observation, notation and calculation. Modernity is defined by an attempt to free the study of being human (ontological questions) from language, so that human beings might be properly interrogated through hierarchical observation, normalizing judgment and the examination. Like Foucault, I am doubtful that such a pursuit will yield the intended results. It is these unintended consequences – the effects of the project

DOI: 10.1057/9781137364791

upon the discursive formation of childhood and our senses of being human – that interests me.

Perhaps a less historical and less religiously loaded analogy might help some grasp the inescapable limits of representation. If *to be* is the canvas upon which all nouns and adjectives rely to colour, define and form statements aligned collectively into discursive structures, a change in the canvas (or *essence)* of language itself (a change in the structure of *to be* or *to become* and its consequences for the child-age-generational complex) cannot be conclusively demonstrated with textual evidence (with what *exists*), anymore than techniques with paint, brush and knife can be used to explore the surface upon which its representations emerge. There is no way around this limitation. We are like Moses when we reach for the historicity of being in time or *age*. We might bring down from the mountain a framework for governing ourselves. Short of the word becoming flesh, we cannot pass over.

If a semantic history of the verb *to be* is unyielding, what might be said?[4] I offer no satisfaction in the religious sense, but can say that medieval and early-modern English speakers possessed a knowledge of and a concern for children's well-being. Yet, the master-servant sense of being in time was profoundly unlike our own. For them, being human was not achieved by becoming an adult. They had no such linear destination to seek. Ordinary life was a continuous, animated, porous existence that sought an alignment with the eternal order of things.

Medieval Europeans "lived close to the inexplicable".[5] They ritually associated earthy things with healing power. The ancients had advised that a colicky infant could be calmed by placing the dung of a goat into its swaddling clothes.[6] A medieval ritual called for the baby to be pulled through a tunnel of soil to stop its crying.[7] The Roman, Pliny the Elder (23–79 AD), instructed nurses and mothers to spit thrice upon a baby at the approach of a stranger to protect it. Recorded Roman custom called for strengthening newborns by bathing them in the urine of a cabbage-eater. By the end of the medieval period, Europeans had categorized at least 50 distinct ailments special to childhood; much of this was based on ancient sources preserved because people wanted their children to survive, to continue to exist, and to live well.[8]

The power of proximity or contact between bodies, the use of relics, or the repeating of movements according to magic numbers appears again and again.[9] Into the early-modern period, infant babies were rolled on the Church altar to prevent rickets, and had their mouths washed with

DOI: 10.1057/9781137364791

holy water to head-off tooth decay. We know of elaborate medieval rituals for encouraging demons to take a "changeling" (a deformed newborn) and return to the world the mother's natural child. Perhaps these beliefs served the function of encouraging greater infant care, lest the newborn be stolen away by fairies. Medieval religious authorities argued that newborns would be deformed if conceived at times when sexual relations were prohibited by the Church. They argued that birth defects could be delivered as punishment for those untoward words whispered during the height of sexual passions. Upon the hermaphrodite body was written a transgression of the cosmic law that separated humanity into male and female.[10] Certainly, English Puritans continued the tradition of trying to understand "monstrous births", in terms of God's Providence and this should remind us that newborn children mattered greatly to parents and others.[11]

More commonly, the Gospels might be read aloud to a mother during delivery to protect her and the child's life. Godparents might kiss the newly baptized under the belfry as drums and rattles sounded the child leaving the Church. This would protect the babe from becoming either mute or deaf.[12] Stories were told of blind children recovering their sight after baptism. The medieval Church taught that the rite was necessary for salvation, as unbaptized children who died would be consigned to limbo. Bibles might be laid about a restless child's head to send it to sleep.[13] Penitential books instructed (regardless of consent) that a boy who had been sodomized by an older boy or a man must do an act of penance to cleanse himself of spiritual pollution.[14] The body was a sign, disease a mark of sin.[15] The head of the sick might be covered as an indication of contrition.[16] A child suffering from parasites might be circled three times while an incantation was recited, "You are a little worm, not entirely grown; You plague me in marrow and bone, you may be white, black, or red; In a quarter of an hour you will be dead."[17]

From a modern perspective, recounting medieval and early-modern child-care practices may induce everything from laughter to anger. But that is not why they matter here. The search for significance, seeing the body as a sign, are marks of the logic of correspondence between the ordinary and the eternal. Their world was not one of the clock, or mechanical cause and effect, but an enchanted one of resemblance, proximity and reversal.[18] Here was a world animated by a weak distinction between an active subject and the passive object with little use for the Enlightenment division, offered by Rousseau's *Emile*, between

DOI: 10.1057/9781137364791

natural consequences and political authority.[19] Nature had yet become something intolerant of Providence, accepting only the rule of general principles which could be discovered through a 'reason' shared by God and Man.[20] Because of this, there was no space or necessity for childhood to be defined as an instrument for achieving what Charles Taylor calls "radical reflexivity" enclosed within internal processes of development configured by personal experiences.[21]

As the previous section argued, the double-sense of being in time (secular-eternal) associated with the terms of master-servant childhood fostered a fascination with analogue. Its ancient sources lay in Greek numerology and the literary parallelism that has been called the "fundamental law" of Hebrew culture.[22] Nothing was sharper for a mind bent toward a search for eternal correspondence than a story of reversal. This was the intellectual setting that supported medieval rituals of carnival such as the feast of the *Boy Bishop* – established in Europe by the twelfth century (a century later in England). By the late fifteenth century "most" English parishes hosted an *Episcopus Puerorum* (*Boy, Child, Barne, Nicolas, Innocents,* or *Scholars* "Bishop") to commemorate the second most important feast of the Christmas season. The *Boy Bishop* ritual took place three days after Christmas at the *Feast of the Holy Innocents* (*Cildamæssedæg* in Anglo-Saxon and *Childermas* in Middle English) when the chosen boy was likely to give a sermon. Ironic reversal was the theme of the season. A boy was elected by the choirboys to lead processions carrying a staff in full vestments, sometimes circulating incense, and perhaps even singing the mass at various ceremonies over as much as the two-month period from early December to early February.[23]

The *Boy Bishop* was a variant of the *Feast of Fools* rituals that appeared among Europeans from late-antiquity until they were greatly curtailed and isolated during the Reformation. Barbara Tuchman's captivating summary deserves to be quoted at length.

> A *dominus festi*, or lord of the revels, was elected from the inferior clergy... ... and choir clerks, mostly ill-educated, ill-paid, and ill-disciplined – whose day it was to turn everything topsy-turvy. They installed their lord as Pope or Bishop or Abbot of Fools in a ceremony of head-shaving accompanied by bawdy talk and lewd acts; dressed him in vestments turned inside out; played dice on the alter and ate black puddings and sausages while mass was celebrated in nonsensical gibberish; swung censers made of old shoes emitting "stinking smoke"; officiated in the various offices of the priest wearing beast masks and dressed as women or minstrels; sang

DOI: 10.1057/9781137364791

obscene songs in the choir; howled and hooted and jangled bells while the "Pope" recited a doggerel benediction ... from the church to parade through the town, drawing the *dominus* in a cart from which he issues mock indulgences while his followers hiss, cackle, jeer, and gesticulate.[24]

The *Boy Bishop's* reign through *Childermas* (the slaughter of the Holy Innocents) displayed some of the burlesque that Tuckman described. As Jane Tolmie points out, the apocryphal dramas of the Herod's massacre were played by cross-dressing all-male casts. A number of the surviving scripts reveal dialogues that would have evoked in close proximity feelings of absurdity, laughter, horror and grief – a series of emotional reversals.[25]

But "burlesque" might not be the best word to capture the sense of shock engender by these rituals. The visual display of a mere boy standing as the Bishop enacted the larger point of the season. The entry of Christ into the world came with a reversal of earthly order. The ritual brought before the eye, the essence of the biblical story of the *Holy Innocents* – the infants who were slaughtered in King Herod's failed attempt to kill the baby Jesus.[26] As Erasmus' *Homily for the Child Jesus* (1512) claimed, their blood had "consecrate[d]" the birth of Christ. Was this not a reversal of the most profound character? Innocent of ability to know or act, babies had died for an omniscient, all-powerful God who in turn would taste death so all humanity could live. What better way was there to reenact the meaning of the feast than to have a boy vested and presiding as the Bishop over an audience that included the canons of the cathedral?[27]

The few surviving sermons delivered by the boys draw out this theme. One from Gloucester begins by admitting that his homily will lack eloquence, but "Speake I must, allthough lyke a child, and stammer owt of this word of God a briefe exhortation". Another boy's sermon delivered at St Paul's in London in the sixteenth century, borrowed the analogical terms found in *The Ages of Man* to explain the mystery of Christian "childship". Man had journeyed through three ages: (1) the "Law of Kind", corresponded to the natural world of the body and the infancy of humanity, (2) the "Law Written", corresponded to the Mosiac Law and Man's youthful failure to obey God, (3) and finally the "Law of Grace" stood as our adulthood corresponding to the justification of Man by Jesus, but beginning with the first martyrs – the holy innocents. Erasmus' sermon (as translated and circulated in England) elaborated further the meaning of having, "A chylde goynge aboute to speake ... of the ineffable chylde Jesus". *Ineffable* indeed was the word for an infant God – unspeakable, unknowable,

DOI: 10.1057/9781137364791

incomprehensible – the word become flesh – the impossible made possible – a reversal of the order of things in the world. The *Boy Bishop* was a reversal of order, displaying "how much Chrystes wysdom is dystaunce from the wysdom of the worlde (the dystaunce is unmeasurable)".[28]

Reading the *Boy Bishop* historically requires that we take seriously the Christian desire to traverse, to reverse, the "dystaunce" or to seek alignment between Christ and the world. This will be impossible unless one can see a boy standing as bishop as an instantiation of a double-sense of time that defined their sense of the relationship between the secular and the eternal. Otherwise, it may read as nothing but rude mockery. At best historians will engage in a search for its social function. As with the concept of "social adulthood" discussed below, explanations that attempt to get around the terms of the biblical discourse itself (to find the pre-discursive base) should be pursued with care. Natalie Zemon Davis and Victor Turner do precisely this. For Davis the implicit question is whether such rituals were revolutionary or merely a means of reinforcing hierarchy. Generally she finds the latter.[29] For Turner, rituals of reversal offer evidence of a profound human play between structure and anti-structure, or order and chaos. Rites of passage are particularly important because they create liminality, release pressure, and grant structures the flexibility necessary to survive and the ability to change.[30]

When considering functionalist treatments of ritual reversal, we should recall the possibility that the modern concept of *revolution* as liberation from order and power is incommensurate with medieval senses of time and existence. The term's older sense denoted a cyclical return or revolving essence of things. When the *Boy Bishop* and *Feast of the Holy Innocents* displayed a thematic centre of "succession, reversal, and substitution", one might be satisfied with the obvious: it was operating in a way that was entirely consistent with the hegemonic Christian theology.[31] Plays that may strike modern readers as sacrilege, bawdy transvestite challenges to the received truth, also extended the New Testament narrative as a whole. They exemplified a medieval fascination with the paradox of the humanity of Christ as child, and a propensity to elaborate upon stories of Jesus as a boy. According to Amy Vines, "the newborn Christ child is always the crucified Savior", and Christmas was significant as a means for lamenting His death and creating "pathetic union with both Mary and Jesus".[32] For this to resonate emotionally, a sense of what Teresa Kenney called "sacramental time" is required: the chronological order of mere existence (secular

DOI: 10.1057/9781137364791

time) must be experienced as subordinate to the sacred essence of Providence (eternity).[33]

For medieval Christians, shocking reversal of their expectations about master-servant childhood and family relations was a manifestation of the divine presence. Stories circulated about non-believers converted by visions of infants within the bread eaten at the rite of Eucharist.[34] Passions and fears sometimes ran riot and gave us the myth of Jewish ritual murder, positioning abused and violated servant-children as Christ figures.[35] In each of these examples, a reversal of master-servant/boy/child hierarchy in ordinary time and place was drawn out to strengthen the chiasmic (AB-BA) structure of the Jesus story: a virgin gives birth; kings present gifts to *filius nullius*; a sensual speechless infant brings the universal logos into the world; the Son of God becomes Man, so the sons of men can become sons of God again, and so on. None of this was "revolutionary", unless Christianity itself is understood as revolutionary in the old sense of the word.

The conclusion that the *Boy Bishop* strengthened a larger architecture of reversal and correspondence is consistent with the canonical and apocryphal writings from which the *Feast of the Holy Innocents* and the *Boy Bishops* had emerged. In its description of the slaughter of the innocents, the Book of Matthew repeated a phrase from Jeremiah to capture the sorrow of the mothers of Israel (represented by the name Rachel) who wept for children never born, or those lost soon in life.[36] This intertextual link encouraged readers to think about the birth of Jesus in Bethlehem as a fulfillment of prophecy that reversed the Hebrew narrative. In Genesis, Rachel was also the name of the wife of Jacob (or Israel); Rachel lamented her empty womb prior to giving birth to Joseph. Of course, Joseph would find refuge in Egypt after his jealous brothers failed to kill him, but his success there would become the means by which all of Israel's children would become bound to servitude in Goshen under the Pharaohs. Prior to this, Rachel would die giving birth to Benjamin outside of Bethlehem.[37] Jesus would be born at the place of Rachel's death before seeking refuge in Egypt from Herod's wrath. Completing the circle, Jesus would return from Egypt to fashion a new covenant that would free all men from bondage to the violence, hatreds and desires of the world.

The previous paragraph summarizes a narrative that is chiasmic – defined by the reversal of order (AB-BA) and the double-sense of ordinary and eternal time. These historically situated structures of thought (rather structure and anti-structure) best explain rituals of reversal such

DOI: 10.1057/9781137364791

as the *Boy Bishop*. Consider the thirst that Christians demonstrated from late-antiquity into the late-medieval centuries for apocryphal stories of the Christ-child. Unsatisfied by the canonical texts they responded by creating infancy Gospels dating from the late second century into the early medieval period.[38] These stories provide additional Rachels – cast as the grieving mother of infants. One apocryphal Rachel, wife of Eleazar, miscarried her child on the night of the Passover, prior to the day of liberation from Egypt. With her own terrible loss she faces great rejoicing among her kin. Another apocryphal Rachel, wife of Jacob in Genesis, dies in a cave outside of Bethlehem so that Mary can give birth to Jesus in this very cave. The point could not be more blunt. From out of the tomb of Rachel's death would arise life everlasting from the womb of Mary.[39] Again, for a mind configured in the search for correspondence, no story could be more seductive than a reversal that brought the order of things into a harmonious whole.

The life given and lost to the world by the canonical and the apocryphal Rachel and Mary carries with it inevitable suffering. Their willingness to endure this brings its reward beyond this world – beyond ordinary human flourishing. Taking up the meaning of the story of the *Holy Innocents*, the Ælfric *Catholic Homilies* (c. 990) spoke directly to mothers of children lost. A modern translation reads:

> Blessed are the wombs which bore them, and the breasts that such as these have sucked. Truly the mothers suffered in their children's martyrdom; the sword that ran through the children's limbs penetrated to the mothers' hearts. And it is necessary that they have equal shares in the eternal reward, when they were companions in the martyrdom.[40]

This was consistent with the opinions of the Christian writers of late-antiquity who saw the story as an example of the requirement to show pious humility in the face of the pain of human existence. Indeed, this was precisely the teaching that gave us the *Boy Bishops* and the *Feast of the Holy Innocents*. In the eleventh and twelfth centuries, several related plays have survived: including *Ordo Rachelis* (Play of Rachel), *Interfectio Puerorum* (Murder of the Children) or *Ludus Innocentium* (Play of the Innocents).[41] These dramas were structured by songs of complaint from Rachel, followed by responses of consolation from angels. One of Rachel's lamentation has been translated: "O sadness! O the rejoicings of fathers and mothers changed/To mournful grief; pour forth weeping of tears." She rejects consolation. How could anyone ask her to hold her peace, she says, "When I have been deprived of my child/[who alone] would show concern from my poverty,/Who would not yield to enemies the narrow boundaries which Jacob acquired for me,/And who was going to be of benefit to his brethren, of whom many, alas my sorrow, I have buried?"[42] The destruction of her means of protection within the community was no small part of her loss. Remember that Jesus fulfilled his task upon the cross by indicating to his apostle John that he should take Mary as his own.[43] Yet, the eternal answer to Rachel's question was resounding. Yes. Parents and children must submit to suffering. You must accept that the power to give and take life lies beyond yourself. A mother must accept that a higher purpose, an essence which precedes her existence, will be served even in the death of the life that extends from her body. This tragic sensibility was enacted in the plays of Rachel's lament. The same idea was there within the sacred heart of Mary – helpless as she stood before her son at Calvary. These plays must have engendered a visceral response for medieval Europeans living in a world where half of all children perished before puberty.

To say the least, "emotional distance" does not speak to the sense of being that resonates from the discourse of childhood associated with the apocryphal Rachel or the *Boy Bishop*. But, this does not mean there is no historical distance between the ancient ontology of correspondence and the discursive formation of modern childhood. The modern propensity to collapse essence into existence by explaining ourselves in terms of the mechanics of our own interiority, makes it difficult to defend the obligations placed upon Rachel and the holy innocents. To complete this thought, grant me the liberty to draw a shamelessly ambitious contrast. Consider Herman Melville's *Moby-Dick* (1851) as a case in point where the narrative of human suffering has been reformulated such that the slaughter of the holy innocents has lost its power of justification.

Melville's Ahab cannot accept the power of the great leviathan to swim beyond his control, to take his leg, or sink his ship.[44] His pursuit of the whale constitutes the ancient sin of rejecting a power beyond and greater than himself. This is the harbinger of death for him and his crew.[45] Along the way Ahab is given many signs to turn away from his will to power, and one of the most critical junctures presents itself at the end of the book when he meets *The Rachel*, a ship searching for a lost son taken by the white whale of God's Providence.[46] The captain of *The Rachel* implores Ahab to join a search for his lost son, asking that Ahab imagine himself in the same position. Ahab accepts the thought experiment, but refuses

DOI: 10.1057/9781137364791

to put matters of ordinary life above his self-appointed duty to torment tormenting itself.

This appears to be an old lesson, but childhood is in a new place. Notice the reversal of the position of childhood relative to the ethics of master-servant subordination? Traditional Christian piety demanded that the twelfth-century *Rachel* quell her lamentations in the name of obedience to God's Will in order to maintain covenant with him. The medieval Rachel does not do this as well as Mary, who might be called the "teacher of the proper way to mourn".[47] Rachel is more like Job; but all three characters embody a common teaching. Melville's nineteenth-century piety would have us pursue *The Rachel's* lost son and return the sacrifice unharmed. The boy should not be given over silently as Abraham gives up Isaac, or with lamentation as with Rachel's children. Such an inversion of the moral of the Judeo-Christian tradition should not surprise us in a modern novel told by Ishmael ("an orphan"). Melville's Ishmael will be the only son saved by *The Rachel* who stands figuratively like the mothers of Israel, as he wrote in the last phrase of *Moby-Dick*: "weeping for her children, because they were not".[48] With these words, Melville echoed the precise wording given in the King James Version for the slaughter of the innocents in the Book of Matthew, and the lamentation of Rachel in Jeremiah. For *Moby-Dick's* modern readers, pursuit of the essence of the divine had collapsed into the well-being of children. Nothing in the book's weighty pages exemplified Ahab's rejection of the former (the Divine Will) better than his refusal to give priority to the latter (the well-being of the lost son in ordinary time). The *existence* of the child in the world had become the *essence* of things, not through the incarnation of God, but through what Viviana Zelizer has called, in a study of very different texts, the "sacralization" of ordinary childhood.[49]

In sum, a modern shift in the child-age-generation complex is obscured by the opacity of the verb *to be*, but its movement has left its trace upon a larger discursive landscape. You might even say that childhood was an important discursive site for a larger reversal in the meaning of being human. In this we find the great historical significance of childhood and a good reason for dedicating oneself to its study.

Let me offer a final reading to help elucidate the deep structure of childhood by comparing the most prominent medieval and modern narratives of emancipation. First, a question: what is the significant difference between the ancient habit of beginning the story of a life

DOI: 10.1057/9781137364791

with a recitation of lineage ("who begot whom"), versus the modern biographical device of assembling anecdotes of an individual's early experiences of conditioning, development, agency or authentic voice?[50] We are after something more than what was noted by Hugh Cunningham: modern biographers write a great deal more about childhood than earlier ones.[51]

Our answer becomes clear when we compare the position of childhood within two narratives of emancipation: Bede's "Life and Miracles of St. Cuthbert" in *Ecclesiastical History of the English People* (c. 731) to Fredrick Douglass' (1818–1895) *Narrative of the Life of Fredrick Douglass, An American Slave* (1845). In Bede's *Lives* the end of childhood was typically marked with a dramatic revelation of God's Will, or by a conversion of the soul to Providence. With Cuthbert, Bede begins by identifying the life of the Saint with a passage from the prophet Jeremiah (*Lamentations* 3: 27–28) praising those who have "borne the yoke from his youth; he shall sit alone, and shall be silent, because he will raise himself above himself".[52] In contrast, Douglass' *Narrative* begins with the fact that masters deny slaves knowledge of their birthdays, reducing it to "planting-time, harvest-time, cherry-time". A slave had "no accurate knowledge of [his] age, never having seen any authentic record containing it".[53]

Douglass' autobiography was one of a number of slave testimonials which attacked human servitude as a form of relationship (not merely the rejection of the enslavement of a particular group as in *Exodus*).[54] Slave-narratives mounted this attack by showing that master-servant relations broke natural affective ties, robbed slaves of their identities as individuals, and corrupted all involved with slavery. Douglass tells us early in his story that his father was a white man who denied his paternity. So too, the demands of plantation labour "separated" Douglass from his mother's care in his infancy. He overcame these elementary insults to his dignity by remaking his manhood. He becomes a self-made man through three key achievements of individual competent agency: gaining literacy, earning a wage, and physically overpowering his harshest master.

In contrast to Douglass' story of emancipation, Bede's Cuthbert becomes a son of God by accepting service to Christ and rejecting slavery to the world. Cuthbert learns to live first with "bent" back and neck under monastic bondage, and later to take-up the solitude of a hermit.[55] This is not to say Bede knew no childhood – children were not "little adults" in his texts. As a child, Cuthbert rejoiced in contending with

DOI: 10.1057/9781137364791

other boys "jumping, running, and wrestling". Bede paraphrased St Paul, telling us that Cuthbert only "knew as a child, he thought as a child". With this phrase Bede has invoked a key element of the hagiographical pantheon by positioning the child in opposition to the Christian.[56] The emancipation of Cuthbert from ordinary time to the order of things (eternal time) happened when he was called to stop his childish play by a boy of only three years of age. When Cuthbert rejected the initial plea, his small messenger fell to the ground weeping. Cuthbert stopped to give comfort, and the "babe" turned as with a vision calling him "priest and prelate!" (a bishop). Here we have speech from the mouth of a babe, a sure sign of Providence.[57] Such a child was "speaking without tongues", asking why "give yourself up to these things which are so opposite your nature and rank...the Lord has appointed you to be a teacher of virtue even to those who are older than yourself".[58] Bede's Cuthbert was *puer senex* (a child with the wisdom of elders) signifying divine intervention which could overturn the expected limits of earthly lives.[59]

The archetype of *puer senex* is canonically found when the boy Jesus is discovered teaching in the temple, and it is located in English medieval apocryphal lyric when the infant Jesus reveals the Paschal mystery to Mary.[60] Here, we have layers of juxtaposition. Some of these apocryphal conversations between Mary and Jesus were delivered as lullabies (from the Middle English *lullen* – to sing a baby to sleep, based on the Latin *lallare*). In the singing of the baby Jesus, Mary learns that she must suffer the loss of her beloved son. The rhythmic comfort of the lullaby at the narrative point of her greatest intimacy with Jesus simultaneously becomes her first confrontation with the Crucifixion.[61] Mary's communication with the infant Jesus allows her to exist at two points in time and to have a part of eternal knowledge.

We might ask what distinguishes the reversals of apocryphal infancy narratives from the paradox offered by Wordsworth at the close of the eighteenth century – *The Child Is Father to the Man*? Part of the difference is based on the unique paradox of God as Man – the child who cannot change. Yet, this is not the whole of it. The romantic child-age-generation discourse that Wordsworth was refashioning allowed him to imagine the birth of the adult from within the process of the child's subjectivity and development. On the contrary, pre-modern literary conventions did not lend themselves well to the exploration of children's subjective realities.[62] The ancient and medieval apocryphal texts deliver a reversal of expected correspondence, but the dynamic is external rather than developmental.

DOI: 10.1057/9781137364791

This is true outside of Christ-child stories. Working from an Augustinian understanding of the self, Bede could not locate moral resources within the individual.[63]

Bede's Cuthbert must sever himself from the limits of childhood to find the *Way*. On the contrary, modern romantic heroes often find their ways by breaking the chains of servile power and reconnecting with their authentic childhood self – in Douglass' case – by recovering a self fractured in childhood slavery. For Douglass, a person's origins lay in two parents, a place of birth, and a date of record: all specific events of ordinary life. His essence is completely captured by the narration of his existence. Early childhood ends with detachment from the mother, and finding one's self is achieved through various forms of internal competencies and controls (intellectual, financial, physical). For Bede, things worth writing about came from the *logos* of the living God who communicates miraculously out of the mouths of babes, curing of swollen knees, quieting of storms at sea, presenting angels, offering life sustaining bread from heaven.[64] Bede's *Lives* revealed the *Way* of communion with the Father, not the liberation of the self in this world. Communion could only happen if childhood attachment to the material and bodily world was shed by accepting the "yoke" of Providence through devotion to a greater master-servant hierarchy of being.

* * *

Comparing the apocryphal Rachel and Melville's *Moby-Dick*, or drawing a contrast between the medieval and modern narratives of emancipation helps us recognize the qualitative gulf separating the terms of master-servant childhood from the landscape of modern childhood. It highlights that we are dealing with issues that are not limited to the treatment of children or the minutiae of social history. Rather the history of childhood pursued as a history of ideas and sentiments renders insights to the most important questions of all: how have people fashioned, and what has given shape to, their sense of becoming and being human? This is the answer to the question implicit on Wickberg's door.

A sense of master-servant relations was the organizing principle of being and becoming in Anglo-Saxon, Middle, and early-modern English. We have documented three interdependent word sets that helped define the terms of this form of childhood: 1) a land-sex-marriage complex, 2) a boy-youth-servant complex, and 3) a child-age-generation complex. By 1500 in England, a patriarchal relationship of dominion and submission

DOI: 10.1057/9781137364791

had come to define the nature of childhood, which served as an herme-neutic for the ambiguous condition of humanity on earth. Its roots could not have been deeper, situated as they were in Aristotelian concept of *paideia* and the Hebrew ideal of pastoral care. Master-servant childhood was a way of caring for children that required a deep sense of belonging and responsibility for children. It was consecrated in the Church's most important rites and festivals, instituted within the inescapable household relations of marriage, service and apprenticeship.

The language of patriarchy that defined interdependent master-servant households represented the marital bond as a transaction between exist-ing houses and as a means for rejuvenating them and maintaining patri-archal control of land, labour, women and younger people. As we have seen, Middle English terms for males, and some of their Anglo-Saxon counterparts, distinguished men by property status; whereas the most common words for females across the entire medieval period, positioned them in terms of sexual experience, sexual availability, marital status and motherhood.

Household property and land possession could not be easily separated from a sense of the self. Households required relations of service that defined the life-course for most young people. The surviving words (*boy, lad, lass, girl*) usually denoted a position of servitude first, but they were rarely debased, servile appellations. Age and gender were secondary meanings. Today this situation is reversed. Age and gender take prec-edence, and the resonant trace of any connotation of service is likely to be heard as an insult.

The words most closely associated with *child, age* and *generation* dur-ing the Middle Ages call us to consider ideas and practices extending beyond master-servant households and into a wider theological and cosmological field of inquiry. At the base of this language group there is a conceptual split, especially well-spoken in Anglo-Saxon terms of childhood, between terms of growth (*cild*) and descent (*bearn*). The idea of growth was subordinate to those of descent, but they required each other. The image of the child could represent human folly and mortality in one sense, while also signifying our capacity to makes sense of the essence of things and seek adoption as children of God.

Under master-servant childhood, the essence of being human could not be achieved by becoming fully, completely, finally – an adult. No such destination of developmental socialization governed the medieval terms of master-servant childhood. A continuous, animated, external search for

DOI: 10.1057/9781137364791

correspondence had structured European discourses on human existence for more than two millennia. Yet, the terms of master-servant childhood were about to become unraveled. Protestant reformers emphasized a pedagogical path to salvation that intensified the ancient structures of master-servant childhood. They attacked the Church with a "spiritualized" household that might purify the world. The space between heaven and earth narrowed as the representational logic of correspondence began to collapse into an increasingly mechanical, atomistic accounting and examination of a person's life. Belief and unbelief encountered new possibilities. This intensified the theological significance of ordinary household relations that had always been part of Christianity, but during the late seventeenth and eighteenth centuries it metastasized into a radical reconfiguration of the sense of being and becoming human which ultimately displaced master-servant relations altogether. Of course, the story of the demise of master-servant childhood is a topic for the next stage of this project.

Notes

1 Foucault did not emphasize the phrase "historical ontology", yet its assumptions developed in his later works, especially Michel Foucault, *The History of Sexuality: Volume I: An Introduction* trans. Robert Hurley (New York, NY: Vintage Books, 1990). For a helpful introduction to the ontological shape of Foucault's works see especially, Todd May, *The Philosophy of Foucault* (Montreal, QB: McGill-Queen's University Press, 2006). The concept of historical ontology has been further developed in Ian Hacking, *Historical Ontology* (Cambridge, MA: Harvard University Press, 2002).

2 Michel Foucault, Michel Foucault, *The Order of Things: An Archaeology of the Human Sciences* (New York, NY: Vintage Books, 1970): 92–104.

3 Exodus 3: 2–4, 14; Tyndale and the KJV used "I am that I am", translation which comes from the Hebrew "Ehyeh asher ehyeh", and in Greek, "ego eimi ho on". It can also be translated as "I am the Being."

4 The analysis of historical syntax poses this question in an alternative way, not explored here. See Mats Ryden and Sverker Brorstom (eds), *The Be/ Have Variation with Intransitives in English, with Special Reference to the Late Modern Period* (Stockholm, Sweden: Almqvist & Wiksell International, 1987); Merja Kyto, "Be vs. Have with Intrasitives in Early Modern English," in *English Historical Linguistics 1992: Papers from the 7th International Conference on English Historical Linguistics, Valencia 22–26 Sept. 1992* edited by Fernandez Francisco, Miguel Fuster, and Juan Jose Calvo, *Current Issues in Linguistic Theory* vol. 113 (1994).

DOI: 10.1057/9781137364791

5   Barbara Tuchman, *A Distant Mirror: The Calamitous 14th Century* (New York, NY: Ballantine Books, 1978): 54.

6   Angel R. Colon, *A History of Children: A Socio-Cultural Survey across Millennium* (Westport, CN: Greenwood Press, 2001): 87.

7   Aron Gurevich, *Medieval Popular Culture: Problems of Belief and Perception* (New York, NY: Cambridge University Press, 1988): 83.

8   Hugh Cunningham, *The Invention of Childhood* (London, UK: BBC Books, 2006): 31.

9   Patricia Healy Wasyliw, *Martyrdom, Murder, and Magic: Child Saints and their Cults in Medieval Europe* (New York, NY: Peter Lang, 2008): 2.

10   Foucault, *The History of Sexuality, Volume I*, 38.

11   Keith Thomas, *Religion and the Decline of Magic* (New York, NY: Scribner, 1971): 109, 124–125, 728, 731–732.

12   Colon, *A History of Children*, 247–249, 284.

13   Thomas, *Religion and the Decline of Magic*, 40–41, 51.

14   Bob Meens, "Children and Confession in the Early Middle Ages," in *The Church and Childhood* edited by Diana Wood (Oxford, UK: Blackwell Publishing, 1994): 62–63.

15   Eamon Duffy, *The Stripping of the Alters* (New Haven, CN: Yale University Press, 1992): 266–298.

16   Georges Duby, "The Aristocratic House in Feudal France," in *A History of Private Life – Vol. II – Revelations of the Medieval World* edited by Georges Duby, trans. Arthur Goldhammer (Cambridge, MA: The Belknap Press of Harvard University Press, 1988): 51–52.

17   Colon, *A History of Children*, 348.

18   Stephen Wilson, *The Magical Universe: Everyday Ritual and Magic in Pre-Modern Europe* (New York, NY: Habledon and London, 2000).

19   Robert Hoppes argued that for Christian Stoicism and Christian Platoism, reason and nature were closely associated because man's true nature (following God's Providence) is to seek a unity between human and divine reason – or "right reason". Baconian empiricism established relocated reason within the observing subject as an instrument for examining objective nature. *Right Reason in the English Renaissance* (Cambridge, MA: Harvard University Press): 160–162.

20   Foucault called this a "de-governmentalized" cosmos which fostered a governmental state. See Michel Foucault's 1978 lectures at the College de France, published later as *Security, Territory, Population*, ed. Michel Senellart; trans. Graham Burchell (New York, NY: Palgrave Macmillan, 2007): 236–237, 349–350.

21   Charles Taylor, *Sources of the Self: The Making of Modern Identity* (Cambridge, MA: Harvard University Press, 1989): 127–142.

22   "Parallelism in Hebrew Poetry," in *The Jewish Encyclopedia* edited by Joseph Jacobs (New York, NY: Funk, 1906): 520–522; Walter Drum, "Parallelism," *The*

DOI: 10.1057/9781137364791

Catholic Encyclopedia; An International Work of Reference on the Constitution, Doctrine, Discipline, and History of the Catholic Church, Volume 11 (New York, NY: The Encyclopedia Press, 1907–12): 473–474. Also see, Ruth apRoberts, "Old Testament Poetry: The Translatable Structure," *PMLA* vol. 92, no. 5 (October 1977): 987–1004.

23   Warren W. Wooden, *Children's Literature of the English Renaissance* (Lexington, KY: The University of Kentucky Press, 1986): 26–28.

24   Barbara Tuchman, *A Distant Mirror: The Calamitous 14th Century* (New York, NY: Ballantine Books, 1978): 32–33.

25   Jane Tolmie, "Spinning Women and Manly Soldiers: Grief and Game in the English Massacre Plays," in *Laments for the Lost in Medieval Literature* edited by Jane Tolmie and M.J. Toswell (Turnhout, Belgium: Brespols Publishers, 2010): 283–298.

26   Paul A. Hayward, "Suffering and Innocence in Latin Sermons for the Feast of the Holy Innocents, c. 400–800," in *The Church and Childhood* edited by Diana Wood (Oxford, UK: Blackwell Publishing, 1994): 70–78. Martin R. Dudley, "Natalis Innocentum: The Holy Innocents in Liturgy and Drama," in *The Church and Childhood* edited by Diana Wood (Oxford, UK: Blackwell Publishing, 1994): 233–242. Colon, *A History of Childhood*, 249–251.

27   Janet Nelson, "Parents, Children, and Church in the earlier Middle Ages," in *The Church and Childhood* edited by Diane Wood (Oxford, UK: Blackwell Publishers, 1994): 89; Shulamith Shahar, "The Boy Bishop's Feast: A Case-study of Church Attitudes towards Children in the High and Late Middle Ages," in *The Church and Childhood* edited by Diane Wood (Oxford, UK: Blackwell Publishers, 1994): 244.

28   Wooden, *Children's Literature*, 32, 34–36.

29   Natalie Zemon Davis, "The Reasons of Misrule," *Society and Culture in Early Modern France* (Stanford University Press, 1975): 97–123.

30   Davis, cited above, reviews Victor Turner, *The Ritual Process: Structure and Anti-Structure* (Ithaca: Cornell University Press, 1969).

31   Theresa Coletti, "Geneology, Sexuality, and Sacred Power: The Saint Anne Dedication of the Digby *Candlemas Day and the Killing of the Children of Israel*," *Journal of Medieval and Early Modern Studies* vol. 29 (Winter 1999): 30.

32   Amy N. Vines, "Lullaby As Lament: Learning to Mourn in the Middle English Nativity Lyrics," in *Laments for the Lost in Medieval Literature* edited by Jame Tolmie and M.J. Toswell (Turnhout, Belgium: Brespols Publishers, 2010): 204.

33   Teresa Marie Anne Kenney, "Aeternity Shutt in a Span: Time in Medieval and Renaissance English Nativity Lyric," (Ph.D. diss., Stanford University, 1993).

34   Thomas, *Religion and the Decline of Magic*, 36–37.

35   On the baby Jesus within the Eucharist see Leah Sinanoglou, "The Christ Child as Sacrifice: A Medieval Tradition and the Corpus Christi Plays," *Speculum* vol. 48, no. 3 (July 1973): 491–509. On ritual murder see John M. McCulloh, "Jewish

DOI: 10.1057/9781137364784

Ritual Murder: William of Norwich, Thomas of Monmouth, and the Early Dissemination of the Myth," *Speculum* vol. 72, no. 3 (July 1997): 698–740. On Christ-plays see Mary Dzon, "Joseph and the Amazing Christ-Child of Late-Medieval Legend," in Albrecht Classen (ed.), *Childhood in the Middle Ages and the Renaissance: The Results of a Paradigm Shift in the History of Mentality* (New York, NY: Walter De Gruyter, 2005): 135–158; Jean E. Jost, "Loving Parents in Middle English Literature," in *Childhood in the Middle Ages and Renaissance: The Results of a Paradigm Shift in the History of Mentality* edited by Albrecht Classen (New York: Walter de Gruyter, 2005): 307–328.

36   Matthew 2:18; Jeremiah 2:15 contain the echoing passages.

37   Genesis 29–31, 35; 48:7.

38   James K. Elliott, *The Apocryphal Jesus: Legends of the Early Church* (New York, NY: Oxford University Press, 1996); and James K. Elliott (ed.), *The Apocryphal New Testament: A Collection of Apocryphal Christian Literature in an English Translation* (New York, NY: Oxford University Press, 1993).

39   An excellent summary of these themes appears in W.M. Temple, "The Weeping Rachel," *Medium Aevum* vol. 28, no. 2 (1959): 81–86.

40   The translation is from Temple, "The Weeping Rachel," 86, and is drawn from Benjamin Thorpe, ed., *The Homilies of the Anglo-Saxon Church* vol. 1 (London: Richard and John E. Taylor, 1844–6): 81–84.

41   Karl Young, *Ordo Rachelis* (Madison, WI: University of Wisconsin Studies in Language and Literature, 1919).

42   Jean E. Jost, "Loving Parents in Middle English Literature," in *Childhood in the Middle Ages and Renaissance: The Results of a Paradigm Shift in the History of Mentality* edited by Albrecht Classen (New York: Walter de Gruyter, 2005): 320–321.

43   John 19: 26–28.

44   William Braswell, "Accuser of the Diety," in *Melville's Religious Thought: An Essay in Interpretation* (New York, NY: Pageant Books, 1958): 57–73.

45   Lawrence Thompson, *Melville's Quarrell with God* (Princeton, NJ: Princeton, 1952).

46   Ilana Pardes, "Rachel's Inconsolable Cry: The Rise of Women's Bibles," chapter 5 in *Melville's Bibles* (Berkeley, CA: University of California Press, 2008): 123–147.

47   Vines, "Lullaby as Lament," 211.

48   See Chapter 128 and the Epilogue in Herman Melville, *Moby-Dick or The Whale* (New York, NY: Harper, 1851).

49   Viviana Zelizer, *Pricing the Priceless Child: The Changing Social Value of Children* (New York, NY: Basic Books, 1985).

50   The observation has been made by many others, but it is put particularly well by Gillian Clark, "The Fathers and the Children," in *The Church and Childhood* edited by Diana Wood (Oxford, UK: Blackwell Publishing, 1994): 14–15.

DOI: 10.1057/9781137364791

51   Cunningham, *The Invention of Childhood*, 33.

52   The Venerable Bede, *Ecclesiastical History of the English Nation*, trans. J.A. Giles (London: J.M. Dent; New York: E.P. Dutton, 1910): 288.

53   Frederick Douglass, *Narrative of the Life of Frederick Douglass, an American Slave, Written by Himself* orig. publ. 1845 (New York: Penguin Books, 1982): 47.

54   The larger point was made in David Brion Davis, *The Problem of Slavery in Western Culture* (Ithaca: Cornell University Press, 1966); also see, Henry Louis Gates, Jr., *The Classic Slave Narratives* (New York: New American Library, 2002): 1–14.

55   Bede, *Ecclesiastical History*, 289; Douglass, *Narrative*, 48.

56   Wasyliw, *Martyrdom, Murder, and Magic*, 1–3; Graham Gould, *The Desert Fathers on Monastic Community* (New York, NY: Oxford University Press, 1993).

57   Edward James, "Childhood and Youth in the Early Middle Ages," in *Youth in the Middle Ages* edited by P.J.P. Goldberg and Felicity Riddy (Woodbridge, UK: York Medieval Press, 2004): 17–18. Psalms 8:2; Matt. 21:16.

58   Cynthia Hahn, "Speaking without Tongues: The Martyr Romanus and Augustine's Theory of Language in Illustrations of Bern Burgerbibliohek Codex 264," in *Images of Sainthood in Medieval Europe* edited by Renate Blumenfeld-Kosinski and Timea Szell (Ithaca, NY: Cornell University Press, 1991): 161–80. Bede, *Ecclesiastical History*, 288–289.

59   John Anthony Burrow, *The Ages of Man: A Study in Medieval Writing and Thought* (New York, NY: Oxford University Press, 1988): 95–99; Nelson, "Parents , Children, and Church," 88–89; Donald Weinstein and Rudolph M. Bell, *Saints and Society: The Two Worlds of Western Christendom* (Chicago, IL: University of Chicago Press, 1982): 19–47.

60   Rosemary Woolf, *The English Religious Lyric in the Middle Ages* (Oxford, UK: Claredon Press, 1968): 144.

61   Vines, "Lullaby As Lament," 211–217.

62   Phyllis Gaffney, *Constructions of Childhood and Youth in Old French Narrative* (Burlington, VT: Ashgate, 2011): 7, 53.

63   Taylor, *Sources of the Self*, 127–142.

64   Thomas, *Religion and the Decline of Magic*, 28–31.

DOI: 10.1057/9781137364791

Select Bibliography

Ariès, Philippe, *Centuries of Childhood: A Social History of Family Life*, translated by Robert Baldick (New York, NY: Vintage Books, 1962).

Back, Hilding, *The Synonyms for "Child," "Boy," "Girl" in Old English: An Etymological-Semasiological Investigation* (Liechtenstein: C.W.K. Gleerup, Lund, 1934).

Brewer, Holly, *By Birth or Consent: Children, Law, and the Anglo-American Revolution in Authority* (Chapel Hill, N.C.: University of North Carolina Press, 2005).

Foucault, Michel, *The Order of Things: An Archaeology of the Human Sciences* (New York, NY: Vintage Books, 1970).

Goldberg, P.J.P. and Felicity Riddy (eds), *Youth in the Middle Ages* (Woodbridge, UK: York Medieval Press, 2004).

Hacking, Ian, *Historical Ontology* (Cambridge, MA: Harvard University Press, 2002).

Hanawalt, Barabara, *Growing Up in Medieval London: The Experience of Childhood in History* (New York, NY: Oxford University Press, 1993).

Hindman, Sandra, "Pieter Bruegel's Children's Games, Folly, and Chance," *The Art History Bulletin* vol. 63, no. 3 (September 1981): 447–475.

Hudson, John, *Land, Law, and Lordship in Anglo-Norman England* (New York, NY: Oxford University Press, 1994).

Kleparski, Grzegorz A., "Churls, Harlots, and Sires: The Semantics of Middle English Synonyms of Man," *Studia Anglica Posnaniensia* vol. 39 (2003): 47–55.

DOI: 10.1057/9781137364791

Lovejoy, Arthur O., *The Great Chain of Being: A Study of the History of an Idea* (Cambridge, MA: Harvard University Press, 1936).

Nagle, D. Brendan, *The Household as the Foundation of Aristotle's Polis* (New York, NY: Cambridge University Press, 2006).

Schultz, James, *The Knowledge of Childhood in the German Middle Ages, 1100–1350* (Philadelphia, PA: University of Pennsylvania Press, 1995).

Sears, Elizabeth, *The Ages of Man: Medieval Interpretations of the Life Cycle* (Princeton, NJ: Princeton University Press, 1986).

Stanley, Eric, "The *familia* in Anglo-Saxon Society: 'Household,' Rather Than 'Family, Home Life,' as Now Understood," *Anglia* vol. 126 no. 1 (2008): 37–64.

Taylor, Charles, *A Secular Age* (Cambridge, MA: Belknap Press of Harvard University Press, 2007).

Temple, W.M., "The Weeping Rachel," *Medium Aevum* vol. 28, no. 2 (1959): 81–86.

Tolmie, Jane and Toswell, M.J. (eds), *Laments for the Lost in Medieval Literature* (Turnhout, Belgium: Brespols Publishers, 2010).

Williams, Raymond, *Keywords: A Vocabulary of Culture and Society*, revised edition (New York, NY: Oxford University Press, 1983).

Wood, Diana (ed.), *The Church and Childhood* (Oxford, UK: Blackwell Publishing, 1994).

DOI: 10.1057/9781137364791

Index

DOI: 10.1057/9781137364791

CPSIA information can be obtained at www.ICGtesting.com
Printed in the USA
LVOW12*1502210214

374698LV00005B/123/P